The Art of
CLASSICAL
GUITAR
PLAYING

The Art of CLASSICAL GUITAR PLAYING

Charles Duncan

SUMMY-BIRCHARD MUSIC
Princeton, New Jersey

Summy-Birchard Music

International Standard Book Number: 0-87487-079-8
Library of Congress Catalog Card Number: 79-57281
©1980 by Birch Tree Group Ltd.
Princeton, New Jersey 08540. All rights reserved.
Printed in the United States of America.

1 3 5 7 9 11 13 15 16 14 12 10 8 6 4 2

Contents

Preface   vii

Chapter One   The Principle of Functional Tension   1

                   Dysfunctional Tension; Functional Tension: Lever-
                   age from the Fingers; Seating; Conclusions

Chapter Two   The Left Hand   13

                   Mechanics of Left-Hand Position; The Bar (Barré,
                   Capotasto, Cejilla); Principles of Movement (I):
                   The Role of the Arm; Dexterity of the Fingers;
                   Principles of Movement (II): The Role of Anticipation

Chapter Three   Right-Hand Position   35

                   Dysfunctional Tensions of the Hand; Forming the
                   Position; Engaging the Nails; Thumb Position;
                   Engaging the Thumbnail; The Value of Preparation

Chapter Four   Nail Filing   50

                   The Thumbnail; The Filing Process; Nail Care

Chapter Five   Articulation   60

Chapter Six   Coordination and Velocity   70

                   Scales; Velocity in Scales; Chords; Homophonic
                   and Contrapuntal Textures

Chapter Seven Expressive Devices   87

         Slurs As Accent; Vibrato; Right-Hand Flourishes;
         Grace, Emphasis, Closure; Rasgueado

Chapter Eight   The Art of Classical Guitar Playing   105

         Refinement of Tone; Contrast of Tone Color;
         Control of Rhythm; Developing the Line: Thinking
         Upbeats; Expressive Nuances: Segovia's Example

Appendix: A Practice Checklist   119

Selected Bibliography   125

Notes   129

Preface

Until about twenty years ago classical guitar students represented a small minority of musicians. Today they number in the thousands. The causes of this renaissance are various. They include certainly, though not exclusively, the commanding influence of Andrés Segovia and his disciples; the almost hypnotic fascination for young people of guitar music in one form or another since about 1960; the increasing notice from the serious musical community; plus the growing availability of high-quality, moderately priced instruments.

However, this renaissance is still a kind of Cinderella success. Despite the new prestige of the guitar, its lack of pedigree is a nagging liability. This is reflected, for example, in the popular misconception that the guitar is "easy," and worse, in the vague, scanty, or conflicting technical information at the higher levels of study. For, notwithstanding the several introductory methods currently available, we still tend to regard the real command of this instrument as a mystery, and those who have achieved it as intuitive prodigies. That they sometimes are, cannot be denied; but this has no bearing upon the needs of those who must progress more deliberately. It also has no bearing upon the fact that in any art, high achievement is usually raised upon a foundation of conscious craft.

My aim in writing this book is to explain what happens in the finest playing and what in turn the student can do to mold his or her playing to that ideal. The book is not a "method" in the usual sense, nor is it addressed to the absolute beginner. It is more nearly a discourse upon those aspects of playing that lie between competence and art and which, if art is the object, point the clearest way to it. The result of a long and often frustrating quest for personal excellence in playing, it is distilled from years of study during which the central concepts took form under the influence of many leading artists, were tested, refined, and then applied—first to myself and then to my students. Although the results have been gratifying, I can make small claim to the discovery of any truly new concepts of technique. What I have discovered and somewhat methodized, and what I hope this book will reveal, are the kinds of things that are known, whether intuitively or consciously, by leading performers of the Segovia school but which are seldom taught systematically.

A number of outstanding teachers and players have read portions of the manuscript in various stages of its evolution: Mario Abril, Carlos Barbosa-Lima, John Duarte, Oscar Ghiglia, Robert Guthrie, Frederic Hand, Michael Lorimer, and Enric Madriguera. I am grateful to them for their encouragement and helpful criticisms. Dr. Edwin Scheibner, Professor of Physics at the Georgia Institute of Technology, generously took time from a busy schedule to check over the mechanical illustrations in chapters 1 and 2. I owe a special debt of gratitude to Dr. Roy Ernst of the Eastman School of Music without whose many acts of kindness this book would not have been written.

I must also acknowledge a general debt to the influence of contemporary thought on the technique of several other instruments (see Bibliography). The instructional literature for woodwinds, strings, and particularly the piano is far more sophisticated than that for the guitar. Not only does it offer a model of what can be done in explaining the technique of an instrument, it actually provides many insights whose pertinence to the guitar is uncanny. The more one reads, the stronger is the conviction that the guitarist's problems are not unique but are confronted in one guise or another by players of many unrelated instruments.

The following discussion is often painstakingly detailed. Unfortunately it must be so, and I make no apology for that. If an apology is needed, it will be for the omission of any detail that might have helped make an idea more visible to the mind's eye of the reader.

CHAPTER ONE

The Principle of Functional Tension

Fine guitar playing always appears effortless. In one way, the appearance is absolutely accurate. In another, it is so deceiving that misunderstandings quite naturally arise in the attempt to explain what really goes on. One of the most widespread of these misunderstandings concerns the meaning of "relaxation."

The value of relaxation is one of those things that is taken for granted by everyone. In social situations, relaxation means freedom from awkwardness. In the act of sitting in a chair, it means the absence of anxiety or bodily stress. In competitive sports, it generally connotes fluency and power of form—and very nearly the same thing in the performance of music. When we see a great artist perform, we feel that his or her art comes from a spontaneous flow of energy and inspiration, and we infer that this is the product of a relaxed mind and body. With certain qualifications, we are right. Then, we reason that to achieve comparable effects we should build our own technique on various strategies of relaxation, mental and physical. We begin by striving to relax the muscles of our hands, arms, and fingers; and that is where we go wrong.

The only living state in which joints are not fixed and muscles tensed is when a person is unconscious. With respect to the playing of any stringed instrument, there must be constant contraction of muscles to transmit energy to the strings. Moreover, to this one can add the continuous expenditure of energy by the brain. The faster, louder, or more complicated the playing, the more muscular and nervous energy expended.

One need only recall the image of a virtuoso pianist at work, literally, during a concerto to see that fine performance cannot be equated merely with the absence of stress. And yet, in piano teaching, "relaxation" theories of playing were very popular in the not-too-distant past. Although they have been largely discredited,[1] clearly there is some causal relation between relaxation and instrumental excellence. The problem is, the order of cause and effect is often obscure. The following analysis by the great piano teacher Arnold Schultz provides the necessary clarification:

> How did the word "relaxation" ever gain such tremendous currency in modern pedagogy? . . . I believe that a general misunderstanding of the significance of highly coordinated movement is the best explanation. . . . A highly coordinated movement is one which fulfills certain mechanical requirements with a minimal expenditure of physiological energy. This economy of energy, however, is the result of good coordination, not the cause. The relaxation school of piano technique has mistaken the result for the cause, and has sought to produce good coordination by economizing energy. It is not an unusual error in kind.[2]

Nor is it peculiar to the piano, or for that matter, the guitar. In a brilliant treatise on cello technique, Gerhard Mantel makes the same point concisely: "Looseness is not primarily the cause, but rather the consequence of a correct form of movement."[3]

Understood properly, then, relaxation is an important but involuntary by-product of disciplined, intelligent study. In another sense, it is also an aspect of sensitive interpretation. As all music is based on cycles of tension and repose, then so must be the bodily mechanisms which produce it. Learning how and where to relax within the music, so to speak, is therefore important for the realization of one's potential as a musician. But relaxation of this musicianly sort is unthinkable without specific, detailed muscular control.

Quite simply stated, not all forms of tension are harmful. Some are absolutely necessary for playing of any sort; others contribute to the refinement of technique. Still others do in fact lessen efficiency, and some result in a virtual collapse of technique. Distinctions are necessary. Broadly speaking, since there is no such thing as performance without exertion, we can better understand the whole problem as a contrast between *functional* tension and *dysfunctional* tension.

DYSFUNCTIONAL TENSION

Dysfunctional forms of tension are largely involuntary, and therefore hard to control by a simple, unspecific command to relax. They come about either because of anxiety during performance—in which case the origin of the tension is *psychological*—or because of irrelevant or superfluous muscle activity, in which case the tension may be thought of as *physiological* in origin.[4]

Dysfunctional tension of the latter kind has some common and obvious forms. It always appears awkward. It includes the hunching of either shoulder (particularly the right), or the holding of the little finger of either hand stiff and extended, or the "winging" (extreme abduction) of the left elbow. In the right hand, it includes flattened knuckles or splayed fingers (sometimes both); it also includes the uncontrolled bobbing up and down of the hand. In the left hand, it includes excessive pressure from the thumb, excessive wrist arch, and sudden jerky movements. It can include an uncontrolled, extraneous tension or movement in any part of the body—grimacing, teeth clenching, torso swaying, unrhythmic foot tapping, and so on. Some of these can be remedied through concentration, others through better study habits and the kinds of practice techniques discussed in this book.

The most vicious sort of tension is entirely psychological in origin—stage fright. But whether the audience is one's teacher or a crowd in a concert hall, a bad case of "nerves" is not merely a state of mind. It is felt in various ways: tightness in the chest and irregular breathing; worse, poor circulation in the extremities, which makes the fingers cold and insensitive; and worse still, tremors of the hand. Unfortunately there is nothing much that can be done about this sort of tension, at least not directly. There is much that can be done indirectly, however.

The really paralytic forms of stage fright do not arise merely from fear of failure. If they did, many major artists would be out of business. It is in a way reassuring to realize that nervous anticipation is a part of performance. Even after over a half-century of concertizing, Artur Rubinstein confides that he still feels nervous before his concerts. (As a matter of fact, a certain amount of nerves can actually enhance a performance.)[5] Rather, it is the fear of failure coupled with the feeling of its almost certain likelihood that brings on panic. That feeling in turn is compounded of various insecurities in preparation, remembered with devilish accuracy by the subconscious mind and balanced in the aggregate against the number of "perfect" performances, with a resulting predictability of failure that amounts to self-fulfilling prophecy.

There is one reliable way out of the trap. That is to develop utter certainty in all aspects of the playing during practice. With the inevitable gain in control comes a parallel gain in self-confidence. This is one of the great truths of musical discipline, the thing that justifies endless effort to induce continuous, sensitive control. In turn certain forms of coordination must be cultivated in each hand through the mutual play of intellect, physical sensation, and sound perception.

FUNCTIONAL TENSION: LEVERAGE FROM THE FINGERS

The secret of good coordination begins in the fact that considerable voluntary tension is required in both hands in order to play at all. The refinement of technique is, in many ways, the process of learning to control the tension, to direct and focus it, and to restrict the energy expended to the smallest amount consistent with the musical requirement. This can all be comprehended under the mechanical principle of efficiency.

Mechanically speaking, the entire arm from shoulder to fingertip is a system of compound levers. Each part moves as the result of leverage from the one next closer to the body, all the way down to the tips of the fingers. The fixation of any given joint as a fulcrum takes the simultaneous contraction of opposed muscle groups. These consist chiefly of two classes of muscles: *flexors,* which lie on the inside of the arm from the biceps to the palm of the hand and which flex, grip, or pull; and *extensors,* which lie on the outside of the arm from the triceps to the back of the hand and which open, straighten, and extend. Any movement of the next member from a given joint is achieved by the action of one or the other of these two groups. The appropriate muscles contract as a result of a nerve impulse; the bones to which the muscles are attached by ligaments move in the direction of the contraction.

Complicated as it is in terms of neural impulses and anatomy, this process can be understood rather simply in mechanical terms as Class III leverage.[6] The three classes of levers are defined by the physical arrangement of the three components of any lever: resistance, or the object to be displaced; force, or the power used to displace resistance; and the fulcrum, or fixed base from which leverage is exerted. The most familiar lever is a Class I type, where the fulcrum is between the force and the resistance (a seesaw or a tire jack, for example). In Class II levers the resistance is between the force and the fulcrum (the wheelbarrow is an example). Levers of the third class are those where force is applied between the fulcrum and the resistance (like the drawbridge):

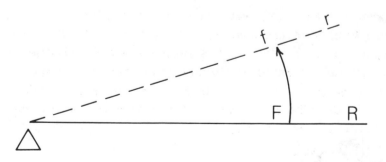

This model of leverage reveals how the various parts of the arm or hand move. Joints serve as fulcra for attached members; force is supplied by muscles whose ligaments attach to the moving part. The biceps flexes the forearm:

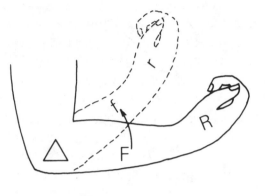

The flexing of a finger is identical if we invert the leverage scheme. A full flex requires all the joints to serve in turn as fulcra for the contraction of the flexor muscles:

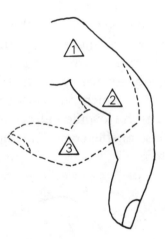

In the movement shown above, resistance consists only of the weight of the finger plus some small friction within the joint. Consequently we have no physical sensation of leverage when merely opening or closing the hand. Supply a real mechanical resistance, however, and the leverage action is felt immediately.

The strings of the guitar, like the keys of a piano, plainly offer mechanical resistance. If we extend our model to include it we will see how energy is transmitted to the strings in either hand.

In the right hand, we can visualize the application of leverage accordingly:

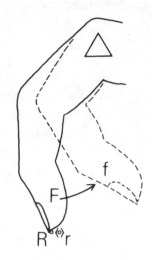

The diagram is simplified for clarity as it shows only one fulcrum, the knuckle joint, whereas the finger is actually a compound lever with the other two joints acting as subsidiary fulcra. There must be joint fixation along the entire finger, otherwise leverage will not be applied effectively against the resistance of the strings.

The exact degree of tension employed at the tip joint is a nice question, however. Relaxation at the tip joint merely shifts the leverage to the middle joint by abandoning the fulcrum nearest the string. The loss in efficiency may be compared to playing baseball with a bat hinged in the middle. A relaxation of the middle joint, which one sees commonly in very young students, pushes the base of the leverage all the way back to the knuckle, with a still more obvious loss in efficiency. The impulse to pluck will move the finger but not the string:

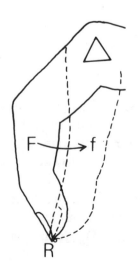

The weakness of this position is apparent in its awkwardness. Before the note is sounded, the finger will have been literally dragged across the string by the sole fulcrum of the knuckle joint.

Does this mean in turn that absolute rigidity of the finger is desirable? Not necessarily. A minute amount of compensatory play at the tip joint is quite possible. It varies between different players, between different fingers on the same hand, or even for the same finger depending on musical context. It has the function of regulating the force at the tip in the subtlest way, for expressive nuance or equality of touch across the hand. The amount of "give" is determined by kinesthetic sensation and should never be confused with a joint collapse which simply does not exist in a disciplined touch.

Although its touch scheme differs greatly from that of the right hand, the left hand obeys very similar mechanical principles. Again, the underlying concept is inverted Class III leverage, as illustrated below:

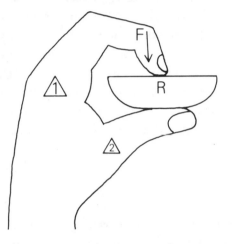

In the case of the left hand, an uncompromising firmness of the fingers is necessary. The collapse of either the tip or middle joint will result in obviously lessened efficiency:

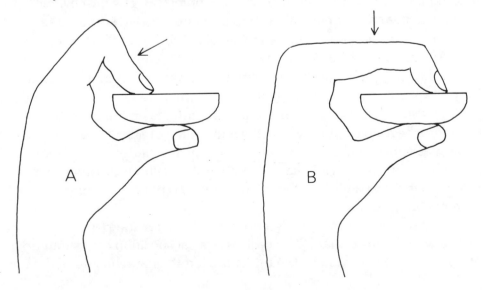

These joint collapses are sometimes practically unavoidable, however. One is common in first finger stops on the higher strings above the twelfth fret; the other, in third-finger reaches across the fingerboard while holding a bar. But such cases should be understood as deviations from the norm of the left-hand finger position. For sound mechanical reasons, this must be an unbroken arch or half-circle—a strong, graceful structural form that, given the anatomy of the hand and the mechanical requirement it faces, transmits energy to the strings by the most direct means possible.

An interesting point of left-hand leverage is the significance of the thumb. The thumb is commonly thought of as an active counterforce to the pressure of the fingers. This is not quite the case; in fact, the thumb should hardly press at all. The primary fulcrum for the action of the left-hand fingers is the same as for the right-hand fingers—namely, the knuckle joint. Counterforce is supplied actually by several sources: the biceps of the left arm, the chest, and the right forearm, in addition to the thumb. The thumb may be thought of as a secondary fulcrum to fix the leverage more securely in the knuckle, to localize the sensations of counterforce, and to stabilize the hand. In reality, however, counterforce is complex, mainly passive, and distributed among different muscle groups. An understanding of this point can help one avoid a common error: excessive pressure by the thumb, with consequent fatigue and loss of left-hand agility.

SEATING

Perhaps surprisingly there is a basic application of the functional tension principle to seating. Beyond the obvious necessity of providing a platform for the instrument to rest upon, what is the point of any given way of sitting? A frequent answer to this question suggests that the objective of seating is repose, both physical and psychological. The best evidence for it would appear to be Segovia's example, where massive authority seems to have, as its physical coefficient, a rock-solid and tranquil posture.

Again, which is cause and which is effect? Common sense bids one realize that Segovia's uniquely authoritative "presence" cannot be accounted for quite so simply. Besides, the variations employed within the standard position itself, plus the occasional major departures from it by artists whose mastery is beyond dispute, suggest that the value of any way of holding the guitar lies substantially in how well it focuses the performer's energy and attention upon the act of playing. A "good" position, in other words, is more active than passive. Rather than a state of repose, it is more accurately an equilibrium of forces.

Any position must provide enough stability for the performer to feel secure with the instrument. The basic "classical" position offers four points of bodily contact: the chest, the top of the left thigh, the inside of the right thigh, and the right forearm. Since other positions offer only three points of contact, that is one very important reason why the majority of performers prefer it. Another lies in the fact that this position permits more bodily symmetry than any other. Note in the photograph the central position on the torso of the instrument in a composition whose symmetry also includes nearly identical articulations of the right and left wrists, elbows, and knees, and the similar angle formed by the elbows and knees:

In this position the legs can provide active support. Note that the left leg points straight to the front, while the right is balanced on the ball of the foot. What the photograph does not reveal is the inward flex of the left thigh necessary to bring the leg into line and to help grip the body of the instrument. Nor does it reveal the springiness in the right leg which comes from the ball of the foot. This also helps to stabilize the instrument by countering the pressure from the right arm, and contributes to a sense of bodily poise. Also, a taut position of the legs is more attractive than when they are allowed to splay.[7]

Another advantage of the standard classical position lies in convenience of access to the fingerboard. This in turn has led to the adoption by most concert-caliber performers of two rather explicit refinements. The first of these is the slight inward inclination of the neck, which simply puts the work closer to the hand that will perform it:

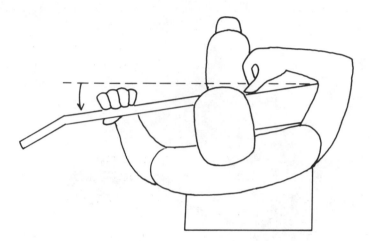

(An outward inclination lessens both the player's physical access to the fingerboard as well as his sense of spatial rapport with it.) The second is the shallow angle that the neck makes with the floor in contrast to the more acute angles possible. The more acute the angle, the more a descending shift will feel like the uphill struggle that it is, in fact; the shallower the angle, the more symmetrical the feel of ascending and descending movements. An angle of about 30—35 degrees from horizontal, as illustrated here and on page 26, represents a nice compromise between the conflicting ideals of a horizontal fingerboard and an erect posture. (It is interesting to note that the flamenco position, which does bring on a rather acute angle, is employed for music confined mainly to one fingerboard position determined by the capo.)

Matters such as the exact height of the chair and stool are secondary. Legends abound concerning Segovia's demands for 7-inch footstools (not 7½!) two hours before concert time. They are part of the colorful but mostly untrue world of musical gossip without which we would be the poorer. The humble portable metal footstand, generally of Japanese manufacture, is the nearest we come to precise control of the variables of seating. It should have flanged feet with rubber caps so as not to rock or slide on polished surfaces. (If the caps tear off, they can be replaced with a few turns of electrical friction tape.) How high one sets it depends upon (1) the height of the chair (lower chair, lower footstool; higher chair, higher footstool); and (2) the length of the torso in relation to the leg (the longer the torso, the higher the footstool, and vice versa). A tall player with a long torso may have to elevate the left leg to the point that the lower bout of the instrument is supported by the top rather than the inside of the right thigh. But this would seem more the exception than the rule. When a player errs in adjusting the footstool, it is usually in making it higher than needed rather than lower. In such cases, there is probably some confusion over the proper amount that the torso should lean.

Lean and *slump* are different. To lean, keep your spine straight and incline your torso forward from the hips and to the left. In the process, your body's center of gravity will shift to the left and the instrument will become more vertically inclined. A positive lean of this sort into the instrument has several advantages. It complements the support of the thighs with a stabilizing force from a third direction. It enhances visual command of the fingerboard. It permits greater freedom of movement of the left arm. In a more subtle way, it also affects the intensity of your playing. To test this, sit back—and notice as you retreat from firm contact not only the loss in terms of physical stability and left-hand access, but also the vague sensations of passivity, uncertainty, and indifference that seem to have displaced the active psychological commitment implied by the more active posture.

The small pressure from the right forearm completes the system. Since most of the task of holding the instrument steady is performed by the legs and body, the support of the instrument by the right arm can be very light. The forearm should feel poised on the edge of the instrument rather than bearing down. Consequently, some shoulder power is necessary to maintain the position. Be sure, however, that you do not hunch your right shoulder; the muscles of the neck and collarbone area stay relaxed, while the deltoid muscle alone keeps the upper arm from slumping. The biceps itself should not touch the instrument. If the biceps is used as the point of support, it must flex continuously to keep the hand in a usable position. Besides the inevitable fatigue of the arm, there will also be a loss of right hand mobility.

The seating position just described constitutes a harmonious synthesis in which forces are counterpoised. It is characterized by strength, balance, and dignity. The position should not be held rigidly. In expressive playing, you may find it natural to lean further into the instrument sometimes, or even to pull back from it upon occasion; to point accents by a nod of the head; to mime a crescendo by a sway of the torso; in other words, to dramatize the music for yourself and for your audience by bodily movement. Together with the various flourishes available to the right hand (see chapter 7), this kind of "body language" relieves stiffness and imparts vitality and visual appeal to a performance. It should not be forced, but by the same token neither should it be inhibited—at least, so long as it is musically relevant movement and not nervous mannerism. The latter tends to be nonrhythmic, physically awkward, and distracting; musically relevant movement, in contrast, is a feature of artistic playing. The physical basis of it is a seated posture that is taut and springy, not inert. Active seating promotes lively performance.

CONCLUSIONS

As an underlying concept of technique, "relaxation" is too vague to be useful—that is, unless the term is used much more precisely than in any broad exhortation to "play relaxed." As often as not, such advice misleads the developing guitarist whose reflexes are still unreliable. Although in the long run, certain inner forms of relaxation are absolutely necessary for artistic playing, mostly they are peripheral to the study of instrumental technique. They have to do rather with the player's confidence, emotional well-being, health, and powers of concentration under stress, plus numerous circumstantial factors. Some performers have experimented with psychoanalysis, with hatha-yoga, or with meditation, among other things, in hope of attaining relaxation. In some cases they have achieved personally satisfying results, but not consistently enough to prove the value for all of any particular program.[8]

On the other hand, certain elementary laws of mechanics and physiology do serve as a universal reference point. This has been emphasized for some time in the best thought on piano and string technique and is just as applicable to the guitar. Fingers that seem to work in a relaxed manner are primarily working in a coordinated manner; actually there is continual expenditure of energy and continual muscular contraction. Because this effort is efficient (that is, uses the smallest work mechanism required by the music), it is not felt as tension. But it is effort, and may therefore be understood more accurately as the product of functional tension, rather than the product of relaxation—which is in fact its most important by-product.

The principle of functional tension includes seating and further entails a variety of practice strategies, the goal of which is a natural, intuitive command of technique. Not all motor mechanisms of technique are accessible to conscious control, but many of them are—more than we usually suspect. There is evidence aplenty that the more of them we can control consciously, the more we can later come to rely upon unconsciously. The problem lies first in correctly identifying those modes of touch that define a superior technique; and second, in devising effective practice forms in order to assimilate them.

CHAPTER TWO

The Left Hand

A fine baritone once observed that in guitar playing, the left hand appeared to be the hand of technique and the right hand, the hand of expression. The remark has the startling clarity that can make a casual observation more illuminating than analysis. Of course the right hand has a technique whose challenges are nearly as great as those for the left hand. Nonetheless, they concern the refinement of just a few practical finger deployments upon the six strings. In contrast, the lateral-longitudinal grid of the fingerboard offers nearly a hundred possible targets for the left hand in any number of single points to four-finger combinations. And while there are frequently differing expressive possibilities in different left-hand fingerings of a given passage (even ignoring the use of vibrato), the original proposition holds true. Of the two hands the left is the workhorse; and it is in that sense that we must first address the use of the left hand.

MECHANICS OF LEFT-HAND POSITION

The underlying physiology of left-hand technique is related to other forms of holding, grasping, and carrying—at least as regards the hand itself; the dexterity requirements of the fingers are in a different though related realm. In most forms of such activity, common sense (or gravity) will put the hand and arm into alignment:

Any significant deviation weakens the grip. The truth of this can quickly be proved by the following test: make a fist, and squeeze your fingers and hand as though you were carrying an imaginary suitcase. Now, still squeezing, flex your hand to the side; then flex it forward, then backward.

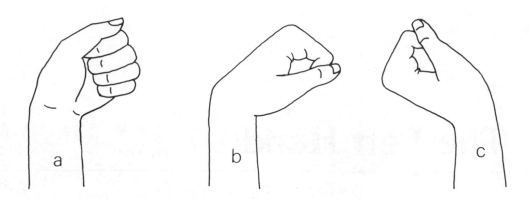

Note in each case the distinct sense of strain and lessening of power. While the physical tasks of guitar playing are not exactly the same as for such tasks as carrying suitcases, essential weaknesses in the position of the left hand occur for much the same reasons they would for some cruder activity. That is, the line of force is broken by the nonalignment of the hand and arm. Muscles that operate the fingers, stretched as they are at the wrist, must flex with less efficiency. Excessive arch can weaken the grip of the fingers by half. Its opposite, the collapsed wrist joint, also results in weakened grip, plus insufficient cross-board reach.

To be sure, small amounts of either are needed from time to time in response to specific musical demands, and the wrist must be flexible enough to respond. For example, in the chord progression below, the wrist will dip inward for the first chord, arch outward for the second:

Sidewise curve of the wrist is also sometimes necessary, as in the case of a severe extension of the fourth finger on the first string. But these minor variations in wrist articulation, continual in good playing, should be understood, and felt, as purposeful, momentary excursions from the basic alignment. The underlying principle of the position and of its necessary minor variations is a law of leverage: force is best applied perpendicular to resistance.

Note in the following illustrations the simple and direct alignment of fingers with each other and with the wrist and arm, the parallel position of the hand with the fingerboard, and the inward slant of the first and fourth fingers. Note too that with tip turned back so that the very slight pressure required can be supplied by the locked joint, the thumb generally opposes the second finger (except for bars, where it will naturally tend to oppose the first finger).

Individual preference will determine the exact point, whether directly opposite the finger or to the right or left of it.

In such a position, pressure will seem to be squarely centered upon the tips for fingers 2 and 3; for fingers 1 and 4, it will be upon the *outside* of each tip. (The callusing of the fingertips will also reflect these differences.) The leaning position of the fingers shown below is distinctly weaker:

Try this test: make a common C chord and allow the fingers to slant leftward, almost to the point of falling down, as in the above photograph. Note the cramping of the fingers and the weakening of the grip, especially in the third finger, which approaches from too far away at an angle, and with poor curvature. Now begin to pivot on the tips, inclining the fingers toward the right until they will go no further. You will note a distinct increase in power as the fingers are brought to bear vertically upon the strings. Correct position also favors the weak third and fourth fingers by bringing them closer to their work and putting the support of the hand directly behind them. The geometrical neatness of the basic position also suggests its mechanical efficiency.

Not all left-hand configurations correspond perfectly to this form, however. Note the impracticality of using it, for example, in making either of the following two common chords:

Here, or whenever fingers are similarly compacted in a close spacing, some outward turn of the hand is natural. This takes a small rotation of the forearm, pivoting from the elbow and on the tip of the thumb:

By the same token, when the fingers return to a more extended spacing, then an inward rotation of the forearm is also natural. To assist in the following chord change for example, the heel of the hand should move inward:

A more or less constant, subtle rotational "play" in the forearm is thus normal in good playing (see also p. 25). Unintentional outward turn of the hand in position shifts is an entirely different matter to which we will return in the discussion of movement. Before that, we must consider another aspect of left hand position which is a subject in itself: the various forms of bar.

THE BAR (BARRÉ, CAPOTASTO, CEJILLA)

Barred chords present certain unique difficulties, even to advanced players. The full bar in particular works at a mechanical disadvantage compared to a curved finger. With the finger fully extended, the joints cannot serve as subsidiary fulcra, and the flexor muscle hence can only partially contract. (Test this by alternately squeezing your forefinger, first extended and then curved, against your thumb and note the difference in the power with which the finger opposes the thumb.) The contrast in leverage between a straight and a curved finger can be diagrammed as follows:

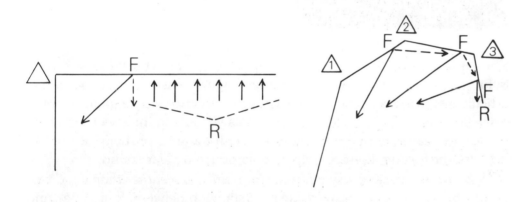

Note in the bar the relative remoteness of force from resistance. By contrast, in the curved finger a flex at each joint both increases the force and makes its transmission to the strings more direct. The difficulty of the full bar is further compounded by variance in the size and shape of fingers and the general musculature of the hand.

There are some general aspects of efficient bar position which we can infer:

1. *A partial contraction between basal and middle segments is better than a completely straight finger.* In the case of very long fingers, all six strings may even be gripped by the middle and tip segments. For a hand of moderate size, the partial flex of the middle joint is still possible:

The value of this for the security of the grip, especially in the lower positions, is hard to overemphasize. First, the leverage is greater since the partial articulation permits some flexor contraction at the middle joint. Second, since the barred finger tends to press on its left side in the lower positions, the above placement permits the bony protuberance of the joint itself to hold the first string, thereby helping to produce a clear sound.

2. *When possible, use a five- or four-string bar rather than a full bar.* Most editions of guitar music make no distinction between four-, five-, and six-string bars.[1] This is unfortunate, because each represents a different sensation and a somewhat different technique. Almost all players will find the partial contraction described above quite easy for a five-string bar. (If the player cannot cover five strings with a partially bent finger, he or she needs a smaller instrument.) Consequently, in most situations where a bar is required as far as the fourth or fifth string, but not the sixth, this form is preferable.

There are exceptions, however. When the next formation is a six-string bar, it is usually better to cover all six strings, even though only four or five are necessary, to simplify the movement to the next position. When a smaller bar puts a sounding string into a "dead space" on the finger, such as the indentation between tip and middle segments, then a larger bar often helps to avoid a buzz by placing the string under a fleshier part of the finger. The full bar may also provide a better base for fingers 3 and 4 in situations such as the following:

Although only the fourth string need be covered, a smaller bar here would push the moving fingers away from their work, weaken their arch, and lessen their reach. A full bar in this case and many like it allows the third and fourth fingers to play more naturally.

   3. *The true half-bar (two or three strings) should be based on full contraction at the middle joint.*

Older methods sometime show the half-bar as a straight finger covering only two or three strings and even caution against bending the finger. Why this advice was ever offered, much less accepted, remains a mystery. The sheer inefficiency of such a position compared to the bent-finger half bar can quickly be proved merely by trying both on the following chord:

The advantage to the third and fourth fingers in ease of access, here and in comparable situations, leaves no doubt as to one major advantage of the bent finger. Another is the better leverage of the bar itself, as shown in the diagram below.

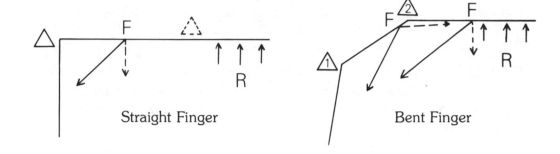

Straight Finger   Bent Finger

In the most efficient small bar the tip segment alone covers the strings to be depressed since this eliminates any wobble occasioned by the hinge of the joint. (For small hands, part of the middle segment may, if fact, be needed to cover three strings.) A corollary is that the small bar is not always confined to the first two or three strings; the collapsed tip segment also may be used to cover lower strings without recourse to the full bar:

PRINCIPLES OF MOVEMENT (I): THE ROLE OF THE ARM

All left-hand movements fall within the categories either of *position* or *shift*. Position movements include lateral exchanges of the fingers, plus one-fret extensions and contractions in which the thumb, although it may pivot quite freely, stays fixed to its point of support on the neck. Shifting movements relocate the thumb, whether by one fret or twelve.

During a shift, this temporary loss of contact plus the need to move quickly from one fret to another creates uncertainty. Careful fingering will help, especially the use of guide fingers. Guide fingers connect one position to another with a slide and serve as a mental and kinesthetic point of reference. Nonetheless, their use, even if quite clever, will not automatically make for effortless shifting; besides, we must often shift without a guide finger to help. The real "secret" of good shifting has to do rather with how we carry the hand from one position to another.

The simple fact to keep always in mind is that the entire mass of the arm must move during a shift. Moreover, this movement comprises both an accelerating phase at its beginning and a braking phase at its end. Since a dead weight of several pounds is involved, the inertial forces are something to be reckoned with. Indeed, if the movement quality of the shift is faulty, the player will unconsciously fight the inertia of the arm, whether as a stationary or a moving mass. It is important, therefore, to understand the kind of movement employed in the most efficient style of shifting.

All shifts are based on either or both of two types of upper-arm movement:

(1) In-and-out movement (adduction-abduction), of the upper arm

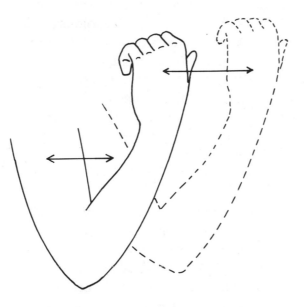

and (2), rotary movement (pronation-supination) of the upper arm:

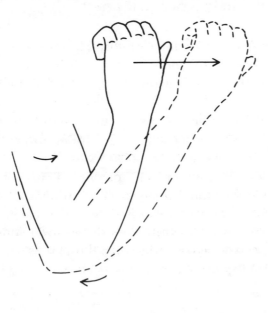

Although either may form the basis of a shift, movements based wholly on one or the other tend to be awkward. The shift based on in-out movement of the upper arm alone is a whole-arm shift in which the hand can move no faster than the upper arm. Therefore, the mass of the arm must accelerate rapidly at the beginning of the shift and be braked at the instant the hand arrives at the new position. The larger the shift, the more sudden the efforts required. This is why shifts done in such fashion seem jerky or stiff.

As an alternative, the shift performed by rotation of the upper arm would seem easier, and in one way it is. A small rotary movement of the bent arm results in a wide arc of movement by the hand, much like the swing of a pendulum. The hand and forearm accelerate passively, with no sense of muscular strain. However, if the acceleration is effortless, the braking effort is if anything even more abrupt than in the whole-arm shift. This is because the slinging character of the movement generates more momentum in the hand than can be controlled without strong countereffort. (Oddly enough, the very thing that renders the movement inappropriate for shifting makes it the basis of a good vibrato; see chapter 7.)

The fact is that effective shifting combines both forms of upper-arm movement, and differently for ascending and descending shifts. In both cases, the idea is to break down the shift into phases for the reason Gerhard Mantel suggests in discussing the very similar technique for the cello:

> If during a position change, the arm moves exactly parallel to the fingers, the movement will be so fast that optimal control is not possible....The movement of a position change will therefore have to be drawn out in time, so that the arm starts moving before the fingers do and the fingers execute their fast movement as the final phase. This way the mass of the arm may be accelerated more slowly since more time is available to transport it from the one position to the next.[2]

Whether ascending or descending therefore, the secret of effortless shifting is that *the elbow leads the hand.*

The descending shift has two clearly defined components:

1. Anticipation. The upper arm moves away from the body.
2. Completion. From its new position, the upper arm rotates, carrying the hand to the appropriate fret.

In practice, the two movements will (or should) fuse into one wavelike motion that carries the hand along without sudden effort. The elbow is sensed as the point of control, and its movement visibly precedes that of the hand. To establish the "inchworm" feel of this two-stage movement, try it on a sequence of easy symmetrical chords such as the following:

The ascending shift is not exactly a mirror image of the descending. In the ascending shift the upper arm draws nearer the body while rotating simultaneously. Since gravity helps in ascending, there is less danger of overacceleration because there is less inertia to overcome. Nevertheless, ascending shifts generally can be enhanced by making the elbow describe a small clockwise curve during the shift. This develops a limited passive momentum of the arm without disturbing the hand. You can get the idea of the free and easy grace of the movement by holding your arm bent and rotating the elbow in a clockwise circle, while the hand remains essentially still.

The anticipation in this case is a tiny outward push of the upper arm that initiates the curve the elbow will follow—a little "backswing," in other words. It tends to be accompanied by some additional wrist arch before the shift, although there should be only one fluid, continuous motion from anticipation to completion. (Try the previous sequence of chords in reverse to establish the feel of arm control in ascending.)

In the case of large shifts, either ascending or descending, the elbow anticipation should come well in advance of the actual hand movement. However, if a shift is merely to a neighboring fret, the role of the arm may be very slight. Such shifts are generally not troublesome anyway, and may seem more natural if thought of as hand-and-wrist shifts only. Still, even a one-fret shift can be a nagging source of error, and when it is, the likely reason is that a sluggish arm has hindered or jarred the hand. The wise thing would seem therefore to be always alert to the possible use of the arm more or less deliberately.

Although the upper arm should never be raised any further than necessary, it must obviously be free to move in and out. In the lower fingerboard area, this will result in the elbow's being some six to ten inches away from the body. There is nothing wrong with that. Hugging the body with the elbow should be avoided just as much as the more obvious fault of "winging."

In the ideal position shift, the fingers keep their general alignment and curvature during movement. A descending chromatic scale along one string is the purest example and can be a valuable exercise in economy of finger movement, guide finger usage, and arm control. Be sure to keep the first finger down throughout the scale as a guide finger:

position IX   V   I

Do not try to "plant" the other three fingers simultaneously following the shifts, but allow them to attack and release in their natural sequence. If the fingers are planted simultaneously, each note is produced in turn by a finger lift. With no relief between consecutive movements, the weak extensor muscles that lift the fingers become overloaded. (This may not be a problem at slow speeds; in fast chromatics of any sort, however, extensor overload is the main deterrent.) On the other hand, make the lift of each finger absolutely minimal. At the moment of shift, the second, third, and fourth fingers should be hovering over the frets they have played; they should be parallel with each other and no more than a half-inch above the fingerboard:

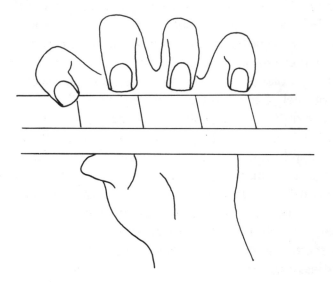

And they should retain this alignment during the shifts. Avoid any outward rotation of the palm or any straightening of the fingers. The emphasis should be upon restraint of movement in extremely slow practice.

We usually think of the work performed within a fingerboard position as the task of the fingers alone, while the arm remains quiet. That this is not entirely the case has already been suggested. The wrist flexes and bends by fractional amounts more or less constantly to give the fingers better leverage, without disturbing the generally columnar form of hand and forearm (p. 14). Also, the forearm pivoting from the elbow naturally rotates in and out to support respectively greater separation or compaction of the fingers (p. 16), again in the interest of better leverage.

A more dramatic use of the entire arm makes large cross-board reaches easier and more natural. It consists of a rotary forearm movement combined with an in or out movement of the upper arm. As in the case of position shifting, the elbow is sensed as the point of control. It moves into the body to support movements of the third and fourth fingers to a lower string, and away from the body to support their movements to a higher string. (Note also in the following example the tendency of the barred first finger to warp back and forth slightly; this "play" in the position is normal and shouldn't be inhibited):

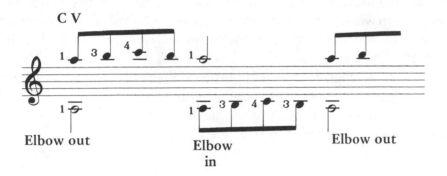

If the third or fourth finger must extend to a higher fret, then wider elbow movements are justified. Extensions on the lower strings may pull the elbow all the way into the body; on the higher strings they take a wide abduction of the upper arm to put the support of the arm directly behind the extended finger. Practical examples of this latter type of spacing abound in the repertoire; here is a well-known one from the *Estudio 17* by Sor (numbers here and below are as in the Belwin-Mills edition of *Twenty Studies by Fernando Sor,* ed. Andrés Segovia):

Shifts of one or two frets that include lateral exchange of the fingers may also be improved by this kind of elbow control. A striking example is found in the *Estudio 9* by Sor:

It helps also in this progression to use a half-bar for the major chords, full bar for the seventh chords. The half-bar yields a much cleaner grip on the first string when the fourth finger is extended; while the clear exchange of one kind of bar for another supports the exchange of fingers and relaxes the hand.

No matter what the movement, there is a natural inclination of the arm appropriate to it. An awareness of the possibilities will contribute much to the fluency of one's left-hand technique.[3] Excursions into the highest fingerboard positions are a special case in point since the main difficulty in playing "over the wood" is a clean entry into and exit from the high position. Finger length will affect its nuances, but the best general attitude of the hand is with the thumb retained at the base of the neck, while the heel of the hand encounters the edge of the upper bout for still further support. The wrist must arch somewhat, but more important is the role of the arm and shoulder. For the arm to support the hand without strain, the left shoulder must dip downward to accommodate the upward movement. Do not hesitate to be dramatic in leaning into the shift.

It helps to have a leftward inclination of the torso already (see page 11); in playing above the twelfth fret, your chin may nearly touch the guitar! The elbow should be well out so that the arm feels free of the body. The following A minor scale on the first string illustrates a typical occasion for the movement:

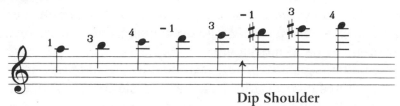

Dip Shoulder

The more rapidly this is played, the more natural it will be to anticipate the dip by a continuous downward-leaning movement throughout the passage.

DEXTERITY OF THE FINGERS

Four requirements underlie the development of finger dexterity:
1. Training fingers to maintain an unbroken arch
2. Increasing lateral separation at the knuckle
3. Developing accurate finger-fall
4. Increasing strength and endurance

In general, the goal of finger development is an agile, balanced hand whose individual fingers are nearly equal in efficiency. Clearly, the main application of the requirements above is to the weak third and fourth fingers. Virtually all dexterity exercises are intended first and foremost to improve the strength, or the separation, or the agility of these fingers.

Among the best of such exercises is the practice of slurs. Beyond their expressive musical value (see chapter 7), slurs have technical value in developing the weak part of the hand. Ascending ("hammer") slurs develop a strong arched finger attack; descending ("pull") slurs improve lateral separation and tip control.

An almost infinite number of slur patterns can be generated from the following:
1. Slurs between the outer fingers (1-4)
2. Slurs between even-odd pairs (1-3, 2-4)
3. Adjacent-finger slurs (1-2, 2-3, 3-4)

The most common practice forms of slurs combine these possibilities variously into exercise patterns along a single string. Such exercises should be performed as follows:
1. Execute the complete pattern in one position, then move to the next (to ninth position, then descend). Reverse the pattern in the descent for variety; use pull slurs instead of hammers, hammers instead of pulls. (The principle is illustrated in the first example that follows.)

2. Hand position should generally be as in the illustration for chromatic scales: knuckles parallel to the fingerboard, fingers arched and close to their respective frets.

3. Play very slowly, for accuracy and decisiveness of attack. Concentrate on the *weight* of impact in hammer slurs. Do not try to stab your finger through the wood; the sensation is more of a fall than a push—the swing of an axe, not a pile-driver. In descending, concentrate on *tip-flex* and restraint of hand movement.

4. Exercise patterns, given on the first string only, should be performed on at least the three highest strings. Descending slurs on any string but the first pose the problem of how to avoid inadvertently sounding the next higher string as part of the follow-through. The solution is to think of such slurs as left-hand rest strokes. Flex the tip straight back so that it rests momentarily against the next higher string, then relaxes upward and away from the fingerboard. At very slow speeds, the stroke will give the sensation "bump-release." Make sure the movement of the release takes place from the knuckle only so that the finger does not straighten.

5. The first finger *always* remains held down as a guide.

The basic pattern for slurs between the outer fingers:

to IX and descend

Between odd-even pairs:

to IX and descend in reverse,
4 2 4 2 | 3 1 3 1

Between adjacent fingers:

to IX and descend
in reverse,
4 3 4 3 | 3 2 3 2 | 2 1 2 1

Somewhat more difficult are triplet slurs—a hammer followed by a pull, or vice versa. Though not very common as accentual patterns in melody, they help consolidate control of the fingers involved. They are also the basis of several kinds of embellishment, such as the mordent and the trill, so that a command of this slur form is necessary.[4] The following two exercises will help develop that command; the first employs adjacent fingers (half steps); the second, the odd-even pairs (whole steps):

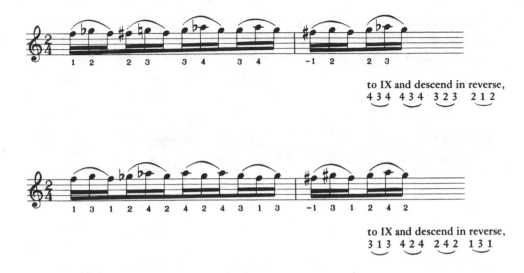

to IX and descend in reverse,
4 3 4   4 3 4   3 2 3   2 1 2

to IX and descend in reverse,
3 1 3   4 2 4   2 4 2   1 3 1

Note in each pattern the extra emphasis upon the fourth finger. The patterns that follow will also help to cultivate the attack of this weak finger. Practice them several times in each position to the ninth; descending with the patterns reversed isn't necessary.

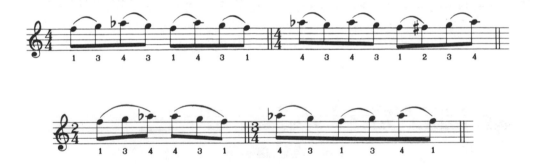

Make sure that your fourth finger attacks and releases without slackening its arch at the tip and middle joints. The pivot for the movement is the knuckle, but the heel of the hand must also participate. First, keep the muscle in the heel of the hand firmly flexed so as to brace and strengthen the finger. Second, in raising the finger to attack, pull the heel of the hand back so that you can support the fall of the finger with the weight of the hand. (Some rotary "play" in the forearm tends to accompany this movement, and shouldn't be inhibited.)

Other common practice patterns for slurs require cross-board movements.[5] Here again, the fingers can be employed in outer, odd-even, or adjacent pairs:

The first of the previous exercises focuses upon the attack of the fourth finger. The second requires mental discipline to disentangle the sensations of alternate-pair attack. The third extends the endurance of the weaker fingers.

Any of the above forms may be practiced from a barred position for even greater challenge. The following pattern, which is a little more elaborate, will suggest the manner of performance:

Another kind of practice for finger dexterity involves the exchange of paired fingers in cross-board movements. This will increase the strength and separation of the fingers if practiced with scrupulous attention to form. One of the best of such exercises is the chromatic octave scale:

A more demanding version of the exercise is in triplets:

etc.

Be sure that finger arch remains unbroken, that fingers extend right up to the metal frets, and that each finger setting is held until the next is in place; otherwise the stretching value of the exercise will be defeated.

Contrapuntal works often afford opportunities for the student to make up his own exercises. The following passage from the Gigue of the *First Lute Suite* by Bach makes a fine separation exercise and, when mastered, will also represent partial mastery of a great piece of music:

One's own repertoire can serve as the basis for many such exercises. Keep in mind when practicing in this fashion that the value of the exercise is directly proportional to the concentration focused upon it. Repetitious practice without proper attention to detail probably does more harm than good. Consequently, here as elsewhere, one must bring an attentive mental attitude to the practice.

PRINCIPLES OF MOVEMENT (II): THE ROLE OF ANTICIPATION

A mechanical-physiological fact that time and again illuminates the guitarist's problems is that curvilinear forms of bodily movement are generally more efficient than angular. This happy correspondence between power and grace is so apparent in sports, and above all in the dance, that we take it for granted. It also happens to be true of the way a fine guitarist's left hand moves.

A poor technique is marked by sudden, stabbing movements, jagged in contour, awkward, wasteful of energy and inaccurate. Faulty position is usually part of the reason, but closer to the root is insufficient anticipation—a fault that always results in abrupt, uncontrolled movement. In a fluent technique there is mental anticipation of each movement, which presets the muscles and "aims" the fingers insofar as this is possible, while the movement itself is marked by economy, precision, curvilinearity, and grace.

The following study procedures may be applied to any piece, exercise, or passage that is memorized. They will help one cultivate a graceful, refined left-hand technique. Do not confuse this sort of practice with playing music. Tempo must be a snail's pace, so that one's attention can focus wholly on the character of the movements.

1. *Never entirely relax the fingers between formations.* Within a fingerboard position, keep the fingers curved (tips pointing to the fingerboard) and reshape them toward the new formation as economically as possible. Do this slowly! Strive for the fluid quality of movement that one associates with slow-motion sports photography. Shifts are the real test of one's control. The untrained hand tends to allow finger spacing to collapse, fingers to straighten, and the palm to rotate outward when quitting a given position. To combat this harmful tendency: (a) pause before each shift; (b) relax the pressure but not the spacing and curve of the fingers; (c) visualize the new formation exactly; (d) anticipate the shift with the appropriate elbow movement; (e) deliberately "carry" the hand to the new position, while (f) molding the fingers into their new formation. Real patience and willpower are necessary to instill this purposeful kind of movement, but the results more than justify the effort. (See also chapter 6, p. 72 ff. and chapter 8, p. 113 for discussion of how the right hand helps the left in shifting.)

2. *Play softly and use no more finger pressure at any time than absolutely necessary.* Most students press harder than they should. This needless tension works against fluency in several ways. First, and most obviously, it hastens the onset of fatigue. Second, the excess friction makes the touch not only generally more sluggish, but also tends to spoil the use of guide fingers by making them topple over during a shift. Third, the hand will seek relief where it can in somewhat desperate relaxations, resulting in loss of position. To keep correct position takes the spacing and curve of disciplined fingers; effort here is offset by the relaxation of finger pressure itself to the minimum necessary to hold the notes cleanly. A light touch can be developed by trying to restrain finger pressure during extremely slow, soft practice. Playing softly is a most important aspect of this training. Because of the sympathetic neural linkage, the left hand automatically works harder when the right hand plays forcefully, and conversely, works less when the right hand plays more softly (see also below, p. 76).

3. *Anticipate each new formation by whatever physical means available; when no physical anticipation is possible, anticipate mentally.* The most direct sort of physical anticipation is through the use of a pivot or guide finger, whether common to consecutive formations or preset to facilitate the change from one formation to another.

common pivot   pivot preset   common guide   guide preset

In addition, there are some less direct but no less valuable methods of physical anticipation. One of the most important is the use of anticipatory elbow movements in shifting discussed above (p. 22). Another takes the form of a conscious effort to "aim" any free fingers towards their next formation before quitting the present one. The beginning of the well-known Bourrée of the *First Lute Suite* by Bach offers some characteristic examples.

While holding the third finger on G at the beginning, have the first finger extended over the second fret for the bar. When *that* is in place, have the third finger hovering over its first string G. When *that* is in place, have the first finger over its F sharp, and so on through the entire piece.

In a light-textured piece, many such overlappings will reveal themselves to sensitive analysis. What about a more chordal structure, where there are fewer free fingers? There still can be mental anticipation. Do not underestimate its value, intangible though it may seem. A clear mental picture of the form the fingers will assume in advance of the movement itself presets the muscles for that movement and makes it much more certain, as if the fingers were pegs dropping smoothly into holes drilled to receive them.[6]

A special application of this point to guide fingers should be noted. To be really effective, a guide finger needs to seem almost like a springboard to the new position—an active, not a passive, link. If it is to do so, then its placement must include a mental anticipation of the shift. This way, the muscles will be preset for the movement. In contrast, if the guide finger is allowed to be merely a passive physical link, its placement will be unrelated to the shift impulse and the shift may falter. Try to think of the finger as truly guiding the hand, not just going along for the ride. Some extra pressure, or "hardening," of the fingertip immediately before the shift often helps. So does dynamic accentuation of the note held by the guide finger, at least when the note is an upbeat to the shift (see also p. 113).

The ideal of left-hand technique is characterized by economy, restrained power, simplicity, and grace of movement—what José Tomás has called with marvelous descriptive conciseness "a quiet hand." The importance of anticipation in attaining this ideal is impossible to overstate. The reader may well agree with this intellectually, but the proof lies in the doing, and that requires patience and will—perhaps even an attitude more common to Oriental philosophy than to the energetic, businesslike Western way of approaching problems. That is, an introspective, detached state of mind; a certain humility before the high demands of self-discipline; and an almost childlike absorption in the doing of a thing, without ulterior motive. To practice the way suggested above while watching the clock and grimly logging one's half-hour of "grinds" is to invite disappointment. The rewards come to those whose approach is more sincere and at the same time more playful. Nothing helps more than a positive attitude.

It also helps to work on music that one wants very much to play. Educators have known for some time that the impact of interest upon learning is decisive. The Bach repertoire contains many pieces of such intrinsic musical worth that they justify any amount of effort lavished upon them. But the piece itself matters less than the individual's commitment to it. More significant is the value of having learned a practice procedure which, when it becomes habitual, is a master key to most of the left-hand difficulties that one will ever encounter.

CHAPTER THREE

Right-Hand Position

Tolstoy's famous remark about families—that the happy ones resemble one another, while each unhappy family is unhappy in its own way—might just as well apply to right-hand position on the guitar. Sound right-hand position is governed by acoustical, mechanical, and physiological considerations. Among fine players, therefore, position tends to be quite similar.[1] Variations are accounted for chiefly by differences in the length and flexibility of the thumb, and even then fall within a pattern determined by function.

In contrast, faulty position assumes a multitude of forms. Sometimes, these may seem natural idiosyncrasies, pointless to criticize or try to change. A closer look usually reveals that they come about through misguided effort, or unconscious tension, or the underemployment of some necessary muscle. (In the latter case, there will also tend to be some excessive muscular contraction elsewhere). Idiosyncrasy has its place in technique, but shouldn't be exaggerated. Instead, we should try to understand how and why faulty position is "wrong" so that we may appreciate why a more correct position is "right."

DYSFUNCTIONAL TENSIONS OF THE HAND

One of the most stubborn tensions of the right hand is the hyper-extended basal segment of the thumb:

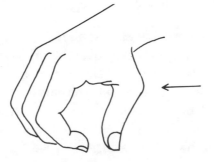

The thumb, because of its separate attachment to the wrist and its rotary capability, permits some variations in acceptable position (see below, p. 45). This is not one of them. It comes about through an unconscious contraction of the extensor muscle, with a corresponding underemployment of the flexor muscle in the ball of the thumb. Its major weakness is that it prevents finesse of attack. Since it is the product of an involuntary muscular contraction, voluntary effort to collapse the protruding joint will be required to overcome it.

Another detrimental form of tension is evidenced by splayed fingers.

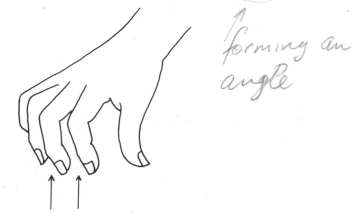

forming an angle

This too is brought on by involuntary muscle contractions that have no playing function. The sense of hand cohesion is vague when fingers are splayed and, at the extreme, there is cramping in the back of the hand. The excess tension in the tips and the consequent angle of attack also make good tone next to impossible.

Collapsed knuckles across the back of the hand accompanied by tightly curled fingers are in much the same category.

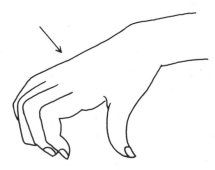

For most playing (and certainly almost all free stroke playing) the knuckle should be positioned nearly vertically over the tip. The only real exception to this rule concerns the practice of rest stroke scales for lightness and velocity (see chapter 6). The further the knuckle retreats from this alignment with the tip, the less force will be available at the tip. With the fingers curled, the leverage of the knuckle is lost, and with it, an important sensation of weight and support from the hand and arm.

Also, as in the case of splayed fingers, the resulting angle of attack yields a comparatively weak free-stroke tone. Why? Because a stroke from this angle displaces the string from the sidewise plane in which much of its natural vibration takes place. The effective transfer of energy from the finger through the string to the top of the guitar is consequently poor. In fact, the more energetic the stroke, the more unmusical the tone:

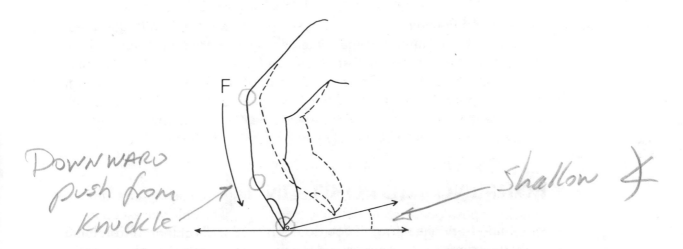

Upward pluck from Middle Joint →

← Greater ∡

Since most guitar playing consists of free-stroke work, a major aim of right-hand technique is a big free-stroke sound. This in turn means a shallow angle of attack, and thus again the desirability of positioning the knuckle approximately over the tip. A free stroke from such a position will resemble rest stroke in its practical effect upon the string. The stroke originates not in an upward pluck from the middle joint, but rather a downward push from the knuckle. (The flex of the middle joint is limited to a short follow-through which barely escapes the next lower string.) Free strokes performed in this manner can actually equal rest strokes in their sonority:

DOWNWARD push from Knuckle

Shallow ∡

Other common forms of dysfunctional tension of the right hand include excessive arch or excessive curvature of the wrist. Muscular strain and inefficient transmission of force characterize both. In the following illustrations, note where the line of force is weakened by the need for muscles to be stretched around a corner to operate the fingers:

Some turn and some arch of the wrist is necessary. The amount varies not only with the individual but also with the musical situation. Still, the positions illustrated above are excessive and weak. Note also in the first how drastically the thumb must extend. A more cohesive thumb-to-finger relationship is preferable. In the second, note that once again the fingers must attack from directly beneath the strings, with consequent loss of tone.

The solution to all of the above problems lies first in understanding the reasons for a correct position, and then in the will to put the position into practice. When a player who already has some command is asked to alter a habitual and apparently workable position, he or she may with good reason ask why. The answer is the same as might be given by a tennis pro if asked why abandon a simple smash serve for the more complicated procedures of good form (the high toss, the reach back, the long swing over the head, putting the weight of the body behind the racket, and so on): these are necessary in order to improve. The desire to improve technique in any physical activity eventually leads to concentration on form.

FORMING THE POSITION

Sit in front of a mirror. If you do not have a wall or door mirror, hang a small mirror on your music stand. Nothing helps insure correct position more than this check from the frontal viewpoint.

1. Make a fist of your right hand; note the contours, especially the pronounced angle between basal segments and the back of the hand:

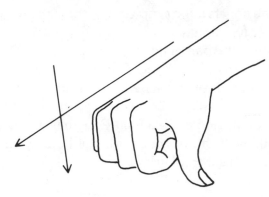

2. Lay the fist upon the strings and uncurl the fingers enough to place the tips upon the treble strings as if to play a three-note chord. Push up from the tips, until the fingers are only slightly curved. Let the wrist follow this movement so that the back of the hand, the wrist, and the forearm are aligned. Raise the wrist a little further until it is gently arched. The position should now appear to you as below:

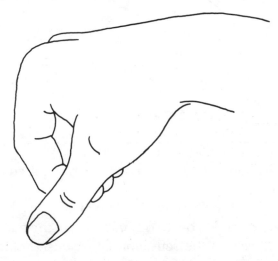

3. Compress the fingers, starting with the little finger, which should be locked against *a* at its tip. Deliberate compression prevents splaying or wobbling of the fingers, even a little of which is a handicap. The *a* finger, for example, poses this problem in many hands:

Compression of the fingers is the simplest way to set the finger into line. But it also serves another function, even for a hand without this problem. Since compression requires the partial flexing of muscles used in playing, it helps activate the mechanisms of the hand. Psychologically, the consequence is the reassuring perception of restrained power and energy.

A device to produce this feeling which, by the way, works wonderfully with beginning students is to place a Ping-Pong ball in the open palm of the hand; grip it lightly with the fingers; and, still holding the ball, place the fingers on the strings, as if to play:

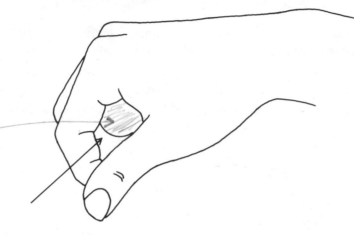

It is possible to execute some movements even while holding the ball, but the value of this little training aid is to form the hand, quickly and with very nearly foolproof accuracy, into an optimal playing position. The curvature of wrist and fingers and the lateral compression required to hold the ball are the same as for firm playing.

Many players find the slight overlapping of tips to be helpful (*a* over *m*, *m* over *i*). The tips will tend to overlap anyway when the hand is placed for a chord; however, to realize the sensation consciously represents just that much more control of position. Especially for players with slender fingers, the value is a firmer grip, reflected in a more robust tone in chords and arpeggios.

ENGAGING THE NAILS

Nails are the final extension of the leverage system constituted by the arm, hand, and fingers. In fact, a fingernail itself can be considered a tiny lever. The more certain its contact, the more efficient its leverage. This means that in theory, at least, seating the nails directly against the strings can be considered an aspect of hand position. In practice, it amounts to a clear mental distinction between the preparation of a stroke and its actual execution.

1. Preparation. Starting from about a quarter of an inch above the string, move the finger downward until the nail directly engages the string while the flesh of the fingertip simultaneously "damps" the string from above.

The sole function of the flesh contact is to minimize any percussive click in the seating of the nail, and there should be no attempt to make the flesh contact actually precede the nail contact (see also below, p. 51). The initial contact between nail and string should be confined to a point on the left side of the nail for normal strokes, as shown in the following diagrams. The first shows the finger from a head-on view, the second from underneath:

2. Execution. From the prepared position, move the finger across the string. This can be accomplished in either of two ways: (a) by a simple flex of the finger, in which case the nail will glance slightly to the right; or (b) by a "slice" to the left, which takes a rotary, propulsive movement of the forearm in support of the stroke. Though sounding more complicated, the latter stroke has an advantage in economy over the first, and is useful to provide accent (see chapters 7 and 8, pp. 98, 109).

The feel of these movements can be established for the two basic kinds of strokes, rest (*apoyando*) and free (*tirando*), as follows:

Rest Stroke. With the thumb resting on the fourth string for support, place *i* on the first string, with the nail securely locked against the string. Again, contact consists of one point only on the left side of the nail.

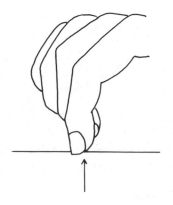

Execute the note by moving the finger across the string either straight in the line of the forearm or by a small throw of the hand to the left which results in the leftward slice of the nail. In either case there will be single-edge contact, and the release point will be approximately at the midpoint of the nail. While *i* is still resting on the second string, place *m* on the first string in prepared position. Execute *m* and, as you do, recover with *i*, returning it to the prepared position.

This is the basic pattern of all alternating strokes. The sensation of exchange and of constant contact with a string may be compared to swinging from hand to hand across the rungs of an overhead ladder. Musically the effect will be that of a gentle staccato:

Free Stroke. With the thumb resting on the sixth string for support, compress the hand laterally so that *i-m-a* form a compact playing unit. Place the fingers on the three highest strings, with the nail of each finger firmly locked against the string:

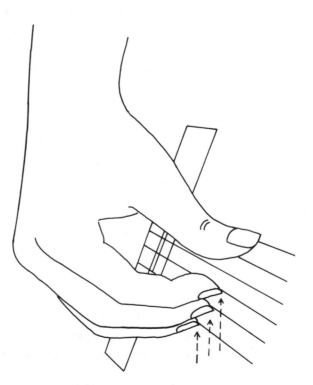

Test the security of the grip by gently squeezing down and in, as if to play. When you are satisfied that the position is secure, execute the notes by pushing down into the strings, and either glancing away to the right rear or toward the left. Good free stroke is not a plucking motion so much as a *push* into the strings with a very slight recoil to the rear. The physical sensation associated with the onset of the sound itself, as opposed to the preparation, should be distinctly that of a *release*. Avoid a large follow-through. The fingertips should move less than an inch, and there should be about the same contraction of joints at the finish of the stroke as at the beginning. (See again the illustration of correct free stroke above on p. 37). Repeat the chord slowly, listening closely to the tone quality. Try to feel as though you were shaping or modeling the tone each time:

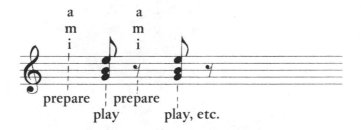

Chords of four notes are the most common. When the thumb is added to make a four-note chord, its preparation is the same as for the fingers. Lock the thumbnail against the string each time at the beginning of the stroke. Balance the down-and-in squeeze of the fingers with an equivalent force from the thumb. The completed stroke should be accompanied by a very satisfying sensation of release. Again, there will be the effect of a gentle staccato:

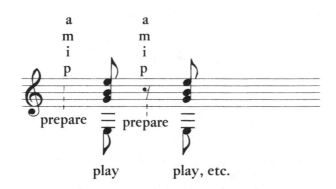

The thumb, however, poses special problems of usage. It can flex in several planes; it can rotate in a circle; its tip flexes independently and can extend backward, in some players to a right angle; and its length in proportion to the fingers varies considerably. Its proper use is therefore a diverse subject.

THUMB POSITION

Good thumb position is based on a tip turned back so as to lie nearly parallel to the string, with a clear presentation of the nail. Furthermore, the wrist should be a full hand span from the face of the guitar in order for the thumb to approach the strings at a useful angle of some 45 degrees:

This position is preferable to a shallow, flattened wrist which makes the thumb approach to the strings more nearly parallel:

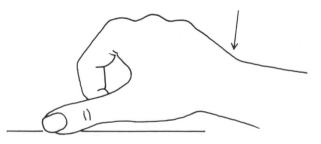

One consequence of the above position is that the thumb clumsily encounters the next lower string with its back and must flex from the tip for the nail to be used. Another is excessive separation of thumb and fingers. Whether in chords, arpeggios, or counterpoint a sense of positive cohesion between the thumb and fingers is a mark of a well-trained right hand. Proper position also encourages the thumb to perform some vital secondary functions. These include damping unwanted basses and serving as a point of support for the movement of fingers alone, as in scales.

Another advantage of the higher wrist is that it facilitates the change from free stroke to rest stroke for the thumb. Just as in the case of the fingers, there should be little difference between the two kinds of stroke, either in appearance or in sound. In the most efficient sort of free stroke the thumb will barely escape the next higher string. Thus, a very small change in wrist position should suffice to make the change from one kind of stroke to the other.

A thumb positioned properly is moved by flexing the ball of the thumb from the wrist joint. There should also be some sensations of tip control, but actual movement from either the tip or middle joints merely complicates the transmission of force and should be avoided. The stroke should be aimed down and to the right, moreover, so as to be a simple flexing movement—the same as that required to grasp a coin between thumb and forefinger. If free stroke, this means that the thumb should come to rest against the tip of the *i* finger rather than higher. In rapid thumb work, the circular path of recovery does impart an outward component to the stroke. There is nothing wrong with that as long as the basic character of the movement is understood to be a flex, not an outward slice. In fact, it may help to think of the thumb describing an oval in repeated free-stroke movements:

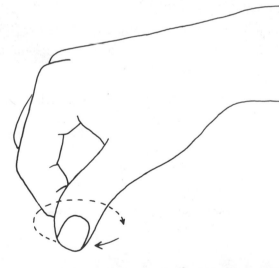

There are legitimate variations to the position described above. In the case of a very long thumb, even with the wrist quite high, there will either be a large separation between thumb and fingers, or an outward lean to the fingers, or both. In the case of a very short thumb, the whole hand may have to lean inward in order to accommodate. Besides the angle of the thumb, observe the difference in angle made by the *i* finger with the strings; the angle formed by thumb and fingers is about the same in either case.[2]

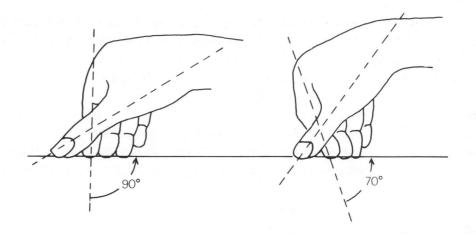

In the case of the thumb which will not turn back at the tip, a larger than ideal separation between the thumb and fingers may be necessary in order to secure a clear presentation of the nail. The reverse is also true. In the case of the player with a "double-jointed" thumb (actually, a weak-jointed thumb) whose tip bends back acutely, some deliberate stiffening of the tip may help to present the nail to the string effectively.

ENGAGING THE THUMBNAIL

The standard method of nail presentation is just the opposite to that of the fingers. That is, the initial contact is near the midpoint of the nail; the release is near the right side (seen from above):

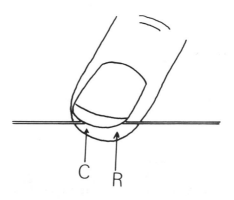

Otherwise, the attack is the same. With the fingers resting for support on the first three strings as if to play a chord, place the thumb in attack position with the nail firmly engaged while the flesh of the tip simultaneously damps; execute the note by aiming the stroke down and to the right, whether free or rest stroke.

There is some variance among fine players in the exact way that the thumbnail engages the string. Partly this has to do with the natural tilt, partly with the length and flexibility of the thumb. Especially, the breadth and arch form of the nail affect one's preference. Furthermore, there is an aesthetic aspect, since changes in tone color require minute alterations in thumb position; strictly speaking, no sensitive player really uses his thumbnail the same way all the time. The diagrams below will suggest the range of possible contrast from one player to the next; they also suggest the extremes of position which may be used by the same player for maximum contrast in tone.

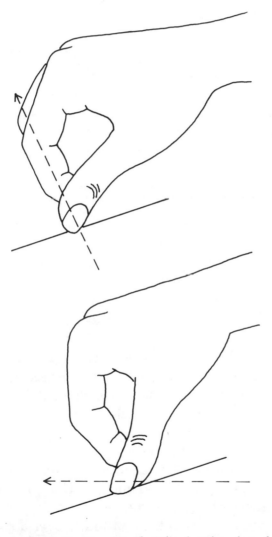

The first position above is associated with a bright, clear free-stroke tone, the second with a darker tone or with rest stroke. This is because as the axis of the nail (the arrows) rotates outward from the first to the second position, nail resistance is lessened; rest stroke becomes more comfortable, and tone, whether rest or free stroke, becomes darker. Conversely, tilting the thumb from the second position to the first increases nail resistance and brightens tone. Between these alternatives, there is a spectrum of nuances (see also p. 108).

However, depending on the particular type of nail and thumb, one position or the other may represent an habitual preference. An interesting aspect of the first illustration is that, at the extreme, it results in an attack that begins not at the midpoint of the nail but at the side. A few players use this touch quite successfully, but most students will do better to cultivate an attack which starts at the center of the nail, with the nail filed according to its natural arch. Since the success of one's thumb technique is so intimately involved with the shape of the nail, the conclusion of this topic must be deferred until the next chapter.

THE VALUE OF PREPARATION

In view of the presumably common origin of string instruments, an analogy from archery seems appropriate to describe the theoretical division of a stroke into phases. The preparation corresponds to notching and drawing, the execution, to aiming and shooting an arrow. Tones that are thought of thus as *releases* of energy will always sound freer and more sonorous than if thought of as expenditures of energy.

It is possible to conceive a third stage to the stroke, the recovery. In the sense of a connective movement that links each execution with the next preparation, it is undeniably part of the overall cycle. But it is not the product of a positive playing impulse. Rather it is a reflex movement and should be as small as possible. Why mention it at all then? For this reason: as we approach the speed limit of our technique, the effort required for recovery increases. Movements become involuntarily larger as the fingers work harder to return to a usable position. The more exaggerated the recovery, the more uncontrolled the playing. At the limits of technique, there are only helpless, flailing recovery movements, which physiologically represent an overload—on the weak extensor muscles in particular and on the nervous system in general.

It is the recovery, then, that imposes an upper limit on velocity. One very important consequence of deliberate preparation lies in learning to overlap the recovery with a preparation impulse. This, more than anything else, will restrict the range of finger movement to the most economical. The gain in accuracy, speed, and sensitivity of touch over a span of several months can be quite phenomenal. This is so for a number of reasons:

1. *Mechanical efficiency.* Execution from a prepared position achieves the most secure coupling of lever and resistance, and consequently the most direct transfer of energy.

2. *Sensitivity of touch.* The resistance of the string can be better

sensed from direct contact at the beginning of the stroke, and upon this sensation the voluntary control of tone largely depends.

3. *Accuracy.* More precise movements are required when the target is limited to a single point on the edge of the nail.

4. *Economy.* Fingers are encouraged to make the small movements desirable from both the mechanical and physiological standpoints.

Does this mean that it is necessary to play always with conscious preparation of notes? Not really. Past a certain speed, which varies with the individual, the sensation of preparatory contact disappears. Preparation and execution come so close together that it is impossible to distinguish them as separate impulses. In the best playing, preparatory contact is constant but fleeting and delicate. It is thus generally below the threshold of awareness, except in the case of heavy articulation or staccato as an expressive device. But it is precisely because the preparatory contact is, or has become, so integral a part of the movement that conscious emphasis of it is superfluous. At this level, touch is regulated by intuition: a complex of tactile and muscular sensations which have through habit become so identified with a given sound that the will to produce the tone automatically invokes the correct movement.

This intuitive form of touch where the ear seems to guide the hand is an attainable goal. But as in most areas of musical discipline, the shortest way is that of patient, conscious application. The truth of this has been eloquently summed up by the great violinist Yehudi Menuhin (who was until his twenties an unreflective, intuitive player):

> Having analyzed and practiced individual movements in great detail, we finally digest and absorb them until they become one smooth, composite and almost subconscious wave. We gradually lose and forget the theoretical scaffolding. This is of course the ideal state provided always that we can return to repair our technical structure whenever it needs it—which is almost every day.[3]

The application of this point extends throughout the range of guitar technique. It is particularly important in the realm of right-hand touch. A prime question, then, for the serious player must be: "By what practice strategies can I develop this kind of touch-security?" It is to that question that chapters 5 and 6 are addressed after an excursion into the subject of nail filing.

CHAPTER FOUR

Nail Filing

Any note on any instrument is a composite of its fundamental plus a number of overtones. Differences in the respective intensities of overtones define the timbres of different instruments.[1] Much of our impression of timbre would seem also to derive from what we hear at the exact moment of onset, for in addition to the overtone signature of a given instrument, there is also a characteristic set of transient overtones at the beginning of a note. These "onset transients" are determined by the method of attack. Experiments with tape recorders and synthesizers have shown that audiences cannot distinguish between a flute, violin, or oboe playing in turn a simple melody when the attack sound of the given instrument has been deleted.[2]

Variations in onset transients not only distinguish timbre from one instrument to another, they also have much to do with the characteristic sound of different players of the same instrument. Furthermore, they define a variety of different kinds of attack, from legato to staccato. (See chapter 5 for discussion of articulations.)

In the case of the guitar, what you hear at the onset of the note is an image in sound of the physical contact. A flesh contact alone will produce a "fleshy" tone, which certainly has its uses as an expressive device but lacks clarity enough to be the norm of good tone.[3] A fashionably pointed nail will produce a hard, angular sound. Thick and thin nails tend to produce tones which are, other considerations aside, "thicker" or "thinner," while a rough nail surface will produce a scratchy tone.

Consequently, the shape and finish of the fingernails largely determine tone quality in the attack. The old argument over whether or not to use nails at all may possibly have stemmed from some harshness in tone quality produced by a majority of nail players when the guitar was strung with gut strings. In any case, the present international standard of tone quality established by Segovia and his more famous students, all of whom use their nails, simply removes the issue from the field of intelligent controversy. In part what we frequently mean by "good tone" is in fact the variety of nuance made possible by different angles of nail presentation. Beyond this, there is one particular sort of nail tone which amounts to a core of sound linking these expressive variations. It is a characteristically bell-like tone that couples expansive sonority with clarity. It can be heard most easily in accented rest strokes performed deliberately and with a slightly angular presentation of the nail (too much angle will produce a muddy tone). If the nail is properly shaped and finished the resulting tone will be splendid.

To determine whether the nail is properly shaped it is best to view it, during and after filing, from a half-profile, as shown below. This allows one to examine the actual contact surface from the point where the nail engages the string to the release point; in other words, to see the nail the way the string sees it.

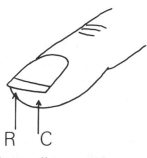

R   C

In general, the contact surface will appear as a straight line (a shallow inward curve if the angle of view is a little lower than that of the illustration). This "ideal" shape will offer gentle, even resistance from contact to release. Any irregularity of line will be felt as an irregularity in the stroke.

A common mistake in nail filing is to curve the edge too acutely. This may result from a misconception of the role of the flesh in producing tone. A player who believes that flesh contact must *precede* nail contact will deliberately file the nail away at the corner and will place his attack further back on the finger. The stroke will consequently incorporate a double impact: first flesh, then nail.

Besides slowing the stroke, this manner of touch, far from producing a soft tone, will inevitably produce a nail click. Over long periods of practice it will tend to wear away the nail at the impact point,

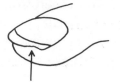

requiring a forced shortening of the nail. Strokes executed in this manner are also rhythmically vague, since the exact flesh impact point will vary by minute quantities from stroke to stroke. Attempts to achieve good tone by this manner of touch are thus self-defeating.

Even if the player has refined his stroke to include simultaneous nail-flesh contact, excessive curve is a drawback. The problem can be readily understood if we compare the needless resistance imposed by excessive curve to the gentler, more even resistance of the blunted form:

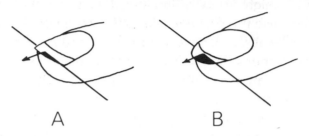

A   B

The difference between the two shaded sections is a measure of the resistance that each nail sets against the stroke. The steep, uphill climb the nail must make in the second illustration will result in either a harsh tone or an uneconomical deflection of the finger to the right in order to escape the unpleasant resistance. The more gentle gradient shown in the first illustration permits—and encourages—a rounder tone. It allows the mass of the nail, the finger, the hand, and even the forearm to be aligned behind the stroke without excess resistance. The efficiency of the energy transfer makes for a sensation, and a sound, of power without effort.

Note that the issue here is not length, but shape; both nails above are the same length. Even though shorter, nails which are acutely contoured will still produce a thin, harsh tone. What then, contour aside, is the proper length of nails? On the average, probably about a sixteenth of an inch, seen from underneath:

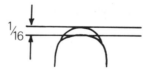

But the average is subject to individual modification, and means little without reference to the specific finger in question—its place on the hand, its size, the relative breadth of the nail, and especially, the arch form of the nail. Nail arch varies not only from player to player but even from one finger to another on the same hand. This means that nails which are properly shaped may look very different indeed when seen from underneath.

The simplest distinction is between nails that are symmetrically arched, but in the one case broad and flattish, in the other, narrow and with a high peak which grows away from the flesh. Seen from beneath, these will appear approximately as shown when properly filed (as elsewhere, the illustration here is intended to typify a general condition and therefore to embrace a number of possible minute, individual variations):

Nails with high arch take a rounder contour seen from beneath; flatter nails take more of a straight line. The distinction is due to the effect of arch on appearance because the first nail is actually longer at the corner than the second. If the nail has a very flat arch, filing on a shallow diagonal eliminates the protruding corner which would otherwise snag the string. However, if the nail has a high arch, a fold of flesh overlaps the corner. Consequently, a less beveled edge is appropriate; in fact, the nail should be somewhat square at the corner. A simple but effective rule is to file the nail in either case so that its edge meets the flesh at the corner. The difference in profile, somewhat exaggerated for clarity, is as seen below (the angle of view is also a little lower than in the first profile illustration above):

Nails with a high arch also need to be a bit longer overall than flattish nails. Why? Because arches always lessen resistance, whereas flat contours increase it. Since nails are often asymmetrically arched, this means furthermore that on any given nail the peak of the arch, whether in the center or to one or the other sides, should be the longest point on the nail seen from underneath. Stated another way, the contour of the nail as seen from underneath should closely parallel the arch form as it is seen from full front.

The typical arch forms (seen from full front) are these:

Only nails with a center peak (*a* above) take a symmetrical filing seen from underneath. If a leftward peaking nail (*b* above) is filed symmetrically from that perspective, it will produce this:

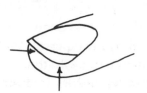

The curvature in the vicinity of the contact point above is excessive but insufficient toward the release point. This will produce a sensation of strong initial resistance followed by an unsatisfying lack of support in the completion of the stroke. The nail will probably feel too short, when it is not overall length but curvature that is the issue. In contrast, if the peak of the arch is on the right side (*c*, p. 53), symmetrical filing as seen from underneath will produce a precisely opposite but equally disappointing result:

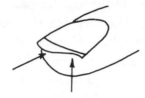

Here, resistance at the start of the stroke is lessened by an arch which, filed too short, has produced a "dip" in the edge. This yields to a "hump" in the flatter portion of the nail, sensed as a snag in completing the stroke. The player may feel in this case that the nail is too long, but again the problem is curvature, not length.

The remedial filing in the above cases requires appropriately asymmetrical contours. Here and elsewhere, the contour, seen from underneath, should correspond quite closely to the arch, as seen from full front. The arch peak, whether in the middle, on the left, or on the right, should be the longest portion of the nail.

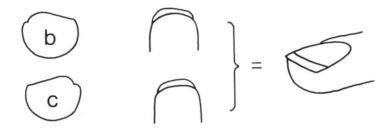

The double arch shown (*d*, p. 53) combines the irregularities of *b* and *c*, hence must combine the remedial shapings. Seen from underneath, the contour should look like a square with rounded corners.

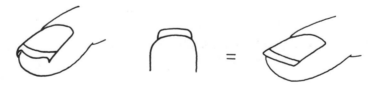

An extreme instance of this arch form occurs when the nail actually hooks downward in the middle. The handicap is not insuperable; some famous guitarists have transcended it. The solution is to blunt the nail enough to eliminate the drastic hump-dip combination. However, in exaggerated cases of this condition, an irregularity in the profile may still remain. If so, some extra leftward lean of the fingers may be necessary to avoid snagging.

The peculiarities of individual nails often reflect the combination of two arch types. For example, from the center peak of *(a)* the nail may slope quite flattishly, as in *(b)* or *(c)*. In such a case, seen from underneath, the nail would appear more pointed when filed properly than a nail with a more rounded arch. Or in the case of arch type *(d)*, one peak may be higher than the other. If so, the line which connects them should slope (seen from underneath), in the manner of arch type *(b)* or *(c)*. Hence, one must experiment to determine which nuances of contour suit one's individual nail type. *In all cases, however, properly filed nails will appear similar when seen in profile.*

No matter what the particular shape, the release point itself (or any portion of the nail past the release point) should be curved gently. Corners will cause trouble. Unless the hand is always held in the same position the angle at which the nail meets the string will vary; rightly so, since this is how contrasts in tone color are achieved. A corner will force the hand to play from the same angle always, thus inhibiting the touch and causing annoyance to the player. The solution is simple: merely round off the corner.

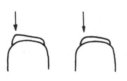

Finally, and again no matter what the particular shape of the nails, a slight staggering of their length is often helpful: *a* a little longer than *m*, *m* a little longer than *i*. The reason is that when the fingers are stacked as for a chord, their most typical position, there are tiny differences in the angles at which the nails engage. If the *a* finger is a good bit shorter than *m*, as it usually is, the difference can be seen and felt:

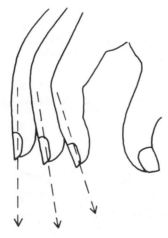

The "bite" of the *i* finger (p. 55) is a little deeper than that of the *m*, and much more so than that of the *a*. Consequently, its nail should be shorter. The respectively greater length of the *m* and *a* nails helps to equalize tone and improve accuracy. This is particularly so for the *a* finger, whose nail should be longest. Remember, however, that any staggering of nail length should be very slight—a matter of a few hundredths of an inch at most.

THE THUMBNAIL

Nail tone in the bass register is essential for clarity. The use of flesh alone by presenting the entire side of the tip to the string occasionally has its uses: in single notes for pizzicato tone, or as a robust chordal accent when swept across the strings (see chapter 7). But these are special effects. Generally speaking, the ensemble between bass and treble is almost always improved by a clearly sculptured bass. Bass lines are heard more distinctly when nail-focused, and their sonority blends better with the treble. Besides the musical advantage, there are purely technical advantages. This is especially so in the case of arpeggios, where the more accurately the thumb is used, the greater the security of the overall movement.

In general, the thumbnail should project about an eighth of an inch beyond the tip—twice the average length of fingernails. But as in the case of fingernails, length is secondary; correct nail shape is determined by the degree and the symmetry of nail arch. Differing shapes are required for nails that are respectively flatter or more arched, and for nails that are asymmetrically arched.

Keeping in mind the direction of the stroke—from the middle of the nail towards the side—the main criterion of thumbnail shape is simple. That is, there must be enough length at the side to offer firm resistance, but without snagging. Consequently, if the nail has a high arch, the shape seen in profile should be squarish, with a full corner.

If the nail has a low arch, it will take a slightly rounder contour in order for the resistance to be softened:

If the nail is asymmetrically arched toward the playing side, it should increase in length toward the corner to compensate for the lessened resistance.

If the nail is asymmetrically arched away from the playing side, the edge should be beveled toward the corner to compensate for the added resistance of the flat contour.

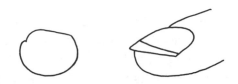

As in the case of the fingers, slight variations in arch (reflecting combined arch types) mean that the exact nuances of the contour must be determined by the individual. Also as in the case of the fingers, a common error in filing the thumbnail is to curve its contour irrespective of the arch form. For a finger this will tend to make for excessive resistance, but in the thumb it will often make the resistance at the release point less than it should be. The result will be either a persistently muddy, unmusical tone, or else an exaggerated position for the thumb, since the player will be forced to reach backward in order to get satisfying nail contact. However, if the nail has been contoured relative to its natural arch, the stroke should have a positive feel of security and finesse, and it should produce a deep, clear tone with several possible shadings.

THE FILING PROCESS

The filing process consists of separate stages of shaping, finishing, and polishing. The materials required for each stage are specific, and in the case of shaping, have to do with the superiority of one type of nail file. The most common file (crosshatch scored blade) literally shreds, and consequently weakens, the nail. The emery board is a partial improvement, but again the essentially abrasive action weakens the edge of the nail and makes finishing problematic. Cutting the nail with clippers avoids fraying the edge, but is an appallingly crude approach to a delicate task.

The best file is a steel file in which the blade is encrusted with fine particles of industrial diamond, or other gemstone. Files of this sort have essentially a cutting, not abrading, action, and they shape the nail neatly without weakening the edge.

To use the file to best advantage, sit with your elbows either on your knees or on a desk or table. The support is important in order both to control the filing movements and to bring the hands to eye level. File the nail on what will appear a straight line, with the file held at an angle to the nail of about 45 degrees.

Make short movements only, and in both directions; the long, single-direction "whisk" of the file used by manicurists is not precise enough. When you have achieved a regular edge, stop filing in this plane and round off the corners you will have created in the process. A stroke or two of the file will be enough to blunt the corner on the playing side; the outside corner may require substantial rounding. Now check from underneath to see if you have approximated the shape appropriate to your arch type. This is also the time to inspect minutely for irregularity in the contour. Eliminate any irregularities you may notice by feather-light strokes of the file from directly above, as in the illustration:

The next stage in filing is finishing, for which you will need a fine grade of commercial emery paper. Number 600 or 500 paper is preferable. Number 400 is acceptable but must be used with some care; you can still alter nail shape with it. A few strokes from underneath (fold and round the paper), from the front and from above eliminate rough places in the filing, filing residue, and the sharp edge produced by the file.

The final stage of the process is polishing. The goal of polishing is a slick, mirrorlike finish to the edge. Either 4/0 jeweler's paper, #500 open-coat silicon carbide paper, Carborundum crocus cloth, or #600 emery paper smeared with vaseline will produce the desired result. All are superior to any type of whetstone, since the paper can be folded and curved for access from any angle. You should use the paper quite freely to polish the nail edge from several directions.

NAIL CARE

Intelligent care of the nails is mandatory for serious guitarists, especially for those whose nails are not strong. If regarded as commonsense preventive maintenance, the subject need not become an obsession.

To begin with, cleanliness of the nails at all times is a good idea. Dirt retains moisture, and that, plus the minute abrasions it causes will weaken the nails.

Some form of liquid supplement to the nails seems worthwhile. There are many nail conditioners on the market that provide a beneficial bath. They contain various nutrients to make the nails more flexible, less prone to exfoliation and cracking. Buffing the nails also stimulates the base of the nail, where all new growth occurs, with an increased blood supply.

Actual breakage of nails (as opposed to their wearing down through neglect, incorrect filing, or faulty right-hand technique) is uncommon for serious players, who by definition try to avoid activities in which nail breakage may be expected. But even the most harmless of pursuits can result in nail fracture; for example, reaching for a doorknob; operating an automobile handbrake; sharpening a pencil; opening a zipper; turning a wet faucet knob; making a bed; dialing a telephone; and others too numerous to mention. In nearly all cases thoughtless routine gesture results in sudden impact, and it is the suddenness of the impact that does the damage. The best preventive against this is to learn to perform such gestures, when it is reasonable to do so, with the left hand. At the least, this will make one more conscious about using the hands, and over a period of time will result in habitual precautions; certainly one of the least glamorous aspects of guitar playing but one with abundantly practical consequences.

Students often believe that a fine sound and optimum right hand technique are the results of correct hand position and properly shaped nails. Would that it were so. The goal is unfortunately more elusive.

Correct position and perfected nail form are only prerequisites. As such, of course, they are critical; one cannot make music on the guitar with poor position and faulty nails. Proper filing and care of the nails is for guitarists the equivalent of bow maintenance for string players and reed selection for wind players. Essential though this may be, it will not amount to very much without intelligent practice: thousands of conscious applications in which an ever more exact use of the fingers is progressively associated with ever more refined expectations of musical effect.

The process of making music, on the guitar or any other instrument, requires constant sensitive control. This is a simple truth, but so comprehensive that the rest of this book is given over to its various aspects.

CHAPTER FIVE

Articulation

The term *articulation* refers in music to the manner in which tones are attacked and released and is distinct from *phrasing*, which pertains more to how they are grouped for expressive purpose. In the main sense, articulation has to do with a player's control of note length, irrespective of written rests. From a staccato which reduces nominal note value by more than half to a legato in which notes are given full value and joined without a perceptible break, there are many possibilities.

The term also can refer, in the technique of winds and strings particularly, to the degree of percussiveness in the attack. Attack quality should not be confused with dynamic intensity; highly articulated notes may be played either loud or soft. Rather, it is more akin to the effect that different consonants have upon the same vowel sound in speech. In this sense, the difference between legato and staccato is roughly the difference between the word *oar* and the word *toe* if either is repeated in sequence. It can be diagrammed as follows:[1]

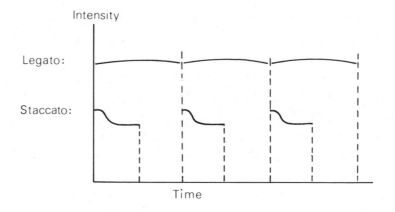

In the case of bowed instruments, legato notes are played under one continuous stroke of the bow. Wind instruments produce their legato by means of an uninterrupted column of air. In either case the difference from notes produced by separate bow strokes or breaths is fundamental. Depending on how percussive they are and the exact technique employed to produce them, these notes have various nuances and go by various names: *martelé, spiccato, détaché,* or *staccato.* They all have this in common: each such note is produced by a separate impulse, has a distinct onset, and is detached in time from the following note.[2]

Common to many authorities on the technique of various instruments is the feeling that a mastery of such articulations goes to the heart of mastering a given instrument's way of producing sound. The following three quotes will serve to illustrate the comprehensive scope of this point:

> The staccato, or short note, is the most basic kind of tongued note. It is the one from which all the other types of tonguing are derived. . . . Beginning players usually find it difficult to play very short notes and their goal will be to make them shorter and shorter over a period of many months.[3]

> The martelé is one of the most fundamental of all strokes, and its mastery will benefit the right hand technique well beyond the limit of the particular bowing. . . . The martelé is decidedly a percussive stroke with a consonant type of sharp accent at the beginning of each stroke and always a rest between strokes.[4]

> Practicing legato passages with staccato touch will engrave more firmly on your memory the order in which the notes (and the fingers which produce those notes) follow each other. . . . Such practicing is tiring to our central nervous system as it requires the finest tonal control along with control over the accompanying sensations. The consequence of such practicing is a feeling of strength in the fingers.[5]

Each author is concerned ultimately with how one develops fluency, precision, legato, singing tone, and so on. But each in his or her own way—an oboist, a violinist, or a pianist—connects that goal with the control of percussive or short-note articulations.

Since the idea apparently spans the range of orchestral instruments, it would seem to be based on common facts of physiology, mechanics, and musical learning. Its relevance to the guitar is certainly quite pointed.

By now, the reader will perhaps have guessed that a true legato is impossible on the guitar. It is simply the nature of the instrument to produce consecutive staccato articulations because of the necessarily percussive mode of attack followed by a rapid note decay. This is no cause for alarm; the same is true of the harp, the harpsichord, and the piano. In each case, a note is percussively formed and thereafter can only die away more or less rapidly. Hence, legato as understood by wind and string players is theoretically impossible for all plucked instruments and even the piano.

The impression of legato is another thing entirely. When asked one time how legato was possible on a staccato instrument such as the harpsichord, Wanda Landowska snapped "My staccato is always legato." This assertion contains an important truth that can be taken to heart by guitarists. The term "legato" itself is somewhat deceptive. Besides a mode of articulation it can also signify a more general impression of connectedness and fluency. In this sense not only is legato possible, it is mandatory if the playing is to be artistic. How then does this elusive effect come about?

First of all, *not* by trying to force a close connection between notes. As often as not, this will result in wooden playing. Neither is legato achieved necessarily by trying to restrain the attack; this may produce weak tone. The impression of legato will best be served by striving for even intensity and perfect rhythmic placement so that all note formations, if not exactly airtight, are perfectly symmetrical. The process of stroke preparation described previously in chapter 3 is the surest, simplest way to achieve this sort of precision in the attack. It follows, then, that a fluent legato style upon the guitar arises more naturally from a command of staccato articulation than from any other means.

If this seems paradoxical, consider the following facts:

1. All notes upon all instruments must be preceded by some silence, however minute. The difference is of degree rather than of kind.

2. All instruments confront similar problems intrinsic to the process of making music: establishing even intensity of tones, controlling tone color where possible, suppressing unwanted non-musical sound, and controlling rhythmic placement. Such problems fall within the scope of articulation.

3. In the case of the guitar, since the only articulations possible are percussive, their refinement must enhance the overall quality of sound. It does so by turning a necessary limitation to musical account. First, the inevitable dead spaces between notes are absorbed into rhythmically exact articulation pauses. Thus controlled, they are perceived by the ear as musical, rather than circumstantial, silences. Furthermore, since the articulation pause masks the finger impact, note beginnings are actually less percussive, gentler sounding, than otherwise.

4. Articulation pauses before notes allow control of color and of rhythmic placement. They enhance the clarity of one's musical enunciation by providing space for notes to "breathe." The pause can be lengthened to create anticipation, as before an accent. It can also be reduced to almost nothing, and, in fact, this is how a real guitar legato comes about. The effort required for preparation is relaxed as the player becomes more secure in touch. He merely gives the fingers the command to "stroke . . . . stroke . . . .

stroke" and listens for even, singing tone. The impression of legato arises quite naturally not only from the lessening of the staccato bite, but also from the sense of additional ease in execution—not from effort but from the relative relaxation of effort.

5. Past a certain speed the articulation pause becomes identical with the time required to produce the note by any method whatever. Furthermore, as velocity increases, staccato articulation itself generally becomes an impression of crisp execution. The value of this in rapid playing cannot be overemphasized and will be discussed in greater detail in the next chapter.

None of the above should be thought a concession to limitations peculiar to the guitar. There are, as we have already seen, enough parallels with the technique of other instruments so that further citation would be cumbersome. One analogy is so relevant, however, that it deserves special mention: the eighteenth-century bow technique described by Leopold Mozart.

> Every tone, even the strongest attack, has a small, even if barely audible softness at the beginning of the stroke; for it would otherwise be no tone but only an unpleasant and unintelligible noise.[6]

Leopold Mozart wrote this some quarter of a century before the innovations in bow design by François Tourte and when the violin was still strung with gut. The stiffer concave modern bow and the use of metal strings have altered instrumental technique. If today a more legato attack than in Leopold Mozart's time is taken for granted, it is because the modern instrument permits and encourages it. The slacker tension of bow and strings in Mozart's day encouraged a greater detaching of notes as a practical necessity which the music of the times made, in effect, a virtue. In a brilliant scholarly treatise on the history of violin technique, David Boyden observes:

> With the old bow, one does not try to achieve an immediate pressure on the string as with the modern bow, but rather to take up first the slight slack, . . . then press quickly into the depth of the string, and relax again. The bow stroke is basically a short one, and the resulting sound is a naturally articulated tone. In rapid figurations a series of these articulated tones resembles a string of pearls since the sound is nuanced, giving the effect of a clear separation of individual tones without the sound of any ceasing completely.[7]

As a description of guitar playing at its best, how apt this is! While it describes a well-executed scale in moderately rapid tempo, its general application will be apparent enough to anyone who has listened intently to the recordings of Parkening, Ghiglia, Williams, or Segovia.

The logical beginning point in the study of articulation on the guitar is not scales, however, but arpeggios. Right-hand cyclical movements may be analyzed without reference to the left hand. Moreover, since in most arpeggios consecutive notes do not fall upon the same string, confusion over the term "staccato" as an expressive device, rather than a practice technique, is less likely than when they do. *The point of note preparation on the guitar is not to shorten but to anticipate.* If the next note falls on the same string, then the preceding note will, of course, be cut short; but the ear and hand should perceive this as an anticipation of the next note. Prepared notes in most arpeggios, falling as they do on adjacent strings, will allow preceding notes to ring. The preparation will thus be felt more than heard.

The simplest arpeggio is the ascending sequence *p-i-m-a:*

p   i   m   a

Simple though it is, it is nonetheless the cornerstone for all ascending arpeggio figures. It is also the basis of one of the most attractive guitar effects, the "rolled" chord (see chapter 7).

To play this, prepare the fingers as if to strike the single chord D-G-B-E. Make sure the nail contact is solid, then apply further down-and-in pressure to take up any slack within the playing mechanism of the hand and strings. Next, by a conscious impulse with each finger, execute the notes of the arpeggio. Make sure each stroke has the character of a *push* more than a *pluck* (see above, p. 37). The execution should feel like a release of energy, not an effort; remember again the analogy of the bow and arrow: how you shoot the arrow by letting go of the string. Restrain the fingers in their follow-through. The more they recoil to the rear, the farther you will have to move them in order to play again.

In slow practice, thumb and fingers should prepare simultaneously. As the arpeggio becomes more fluent, the preparation of thumb and fingers will separate slightly in order to accommodate the *a* finger's preceding execution. (All three fingers should still prepare as one). Use the rest stroke with your thumb, too, when playing the lowest two strings, to help steady the hand in slow practice (at high speeds, rest stroke thumb is impractical in this arpeggio). Be especially attentive to what happens when you play the *m* finger. By this time, your *a* finger may have forgotten its mission and retreated from its post. Repeat the arpeggio until you have conquered any tendency for the *a* finger to lift away from its prepared position when *m* plays.

Any common chord progression will do for the practice of this arpeggio. The Villa-Lobos Fourth Prelude contains an elaborate example, and the guitarist wishing to play this piece will be amply rewarded by practicing in the manner outlined above.

The arpeggio formula below grows out of the simple *p-i-m-a*. Probably the most common of all, it is the basis of several studies by Aguado, Giuliani and Villa-Lobos, and also shows up in modified form in a variety of places.

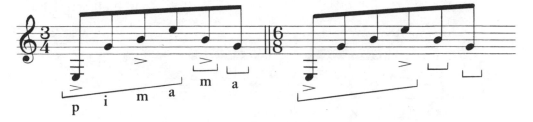

As indicated, there are two possible metric accentuations. The $\frac{6}{8}$ accentuation is both faster and more common.

A player with solid technique should be able to play this figure with $\frac{3}{4}$ accentuation at $\dot{\downarrow} = 96$, and with $\frac{6}{8}$ accentuation at $\dot{\downarrow} = 120$. The surest way to attain this velocity is through preparing the strokes as shown by the brackets. The first four notes are simply the ascending *p-i-m-a* figure and take the same preparation. As each finger plays in the ascending sequence, the ones remaining stay in place until summoned. They must retain their active nail-string contact or the effect will be lost. The last two notes, *m* and *i* descending, must themselves be prepared individually because no descending arpeggio figures can be prepared as a group, either here or elsewhere. Prepare each note as a single free stroke by pushing the finger into the string with an impulse distinct from the actual execution. This movement ensures accuracy and economy, so that the stroke itself is felt as short, powerful, and efficient.

The general rule of arpeggio articulations is to prepare all clear ascending figures as a single group and to treat descending figures as individual notes. The application of this principle to some of the various kinds of arpeggios is shown below by brackets:

(Isaac Albeniz, "Leyenda")

(Dionisio Aguado, Etude I)

p i m a m i m i p i p i

(J.S. Bach, Prelude for Lute)

p m i p a m p m i p a m

(Fernando Sor, Estudio 19)

p i m a i m a i m p i m

(Matteo Carcassi, Etude 3)

The last example represents a large class of compositions where a melody is carried as the highest note of an arpeggio. Usually, in such cases the *a* finger plays the melody rest stroke and prepares together with *p-i-m* only when to do so will not mask a preceding melody note. In the Carcassi this is possible only at the beginning of each measure. When the *a* finger plays its second note, it must prepare as for a single note rather than for a group. An analogous technique applies to Sor's Estudio 17 and Tárrega's "Estudio Brillante," among other pieces.

The Villa-Lobos Etude 1 contains probably the most elaborate arpeggio formula in our literature. The bracketing below will reveal some interesting things about this arpeggio, including why it tends to drag or even fall apart in the third beat (the arpeggio formula is indicated as for open strings).

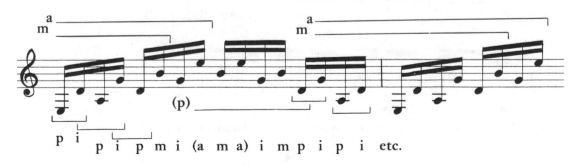

p i p i p m i (a m a) i m p i p i etc.

1. The *a* and *m* fingers can prepare in the last beat of the preceding measure for their first notes in the next. Besides taking care of the preparation, the more or less continual presence of these fingers on the first two strings steadies the hand.

2. The use of the rest-stroke thumb throughout the first beat prepares the second and third thumb strokes (the overlapped brackets). Also, after having played at the beginning of the second beat, the thumb can return to the fourth string to prepare its next stroke and to steady the hand.

3. The *i* finger in the first and fourth beats can generally be prepared together with the preceding thumb stroke; in the second half of the first beat, the thumb preparation will come sooner because of the rest stroke, but *i* still prepares in advance and seems coordinated with *p*. The *i-m* pairing in the third beat is similar.

Basically, therefore, the notes may be prepared throughout in a variety of overlapped groupings, with one glaring exception. The *a-m-a* alternation linking the end of the second beat with the beginning of the third prevents the simultaneous preparation of *a* and *m* at the beginning of the third beat. Consequently, at this point *a* tends to flail and the arpeggio to falter.

The solution is not to refinger the arpeggio for *p-i-m* alone in order to spare the weak *a* finger. To do so will rob the etude of much of its value as a hand developer. Instead, cultivate a sudden, decisive preparation of *a* as *m* makes its stroke. The *a* finger should feel as though it were literally tied to *m*, which pulls it into position as by an invisible string. In point of fact, the two fingers share an overlapped movement impulse: execute *m*/prepare *a*. This, together with the use of the preparations indicated by brackets above, will help condition the reflexes necessary to play the etude fluently. Practice as slowly as necessary to achieve the mechanics and the sensations of control exactly; a metronome setting of $\downarrow$ = 40 is probably much too fast at the beginning. When you can play at $\downarrow$ = 108 with full sensations of control, you should be able to rely upon reflexes for a more brilliant effect at $\downarrow$ = 120+.

The movement described above for the simultaneous "execute *m*/ prepare *a*" impulse is the basis of a successful *p-a-m-i* tremolo. Tremolo pieces such as Tárrega's "Recuerdos de la Alhambra" are among the most charming items in the repertoire. They always please when well played, yet few guitarists below the major artist level seem able to exploit their program potential. The tremolo is not really that difficult to master if its essential timing is understood and practiced accordingly.

In the *a-m-i* sequence of the tremolo, there are two overlapped execute-prepare impulses. As *a* plays, *m* should fall smartly into its prepared position; as *m* plays, *i* should do likewise. Just as in the problem spot of the Villa-Lobos Etude 1, the sensation is of one finger pulling the next by an invisible string. Mechanically, this practice technique binds the execution of each note securely to the onset of the next. Musically, the effect is a dry staccatissimo.

The preparation of *p* at the moment *i* plays completes the pattern—or almost. What about *a*? In very slow practice, it prepares together with the thumb because, as in an arpeggio, the ascending direction permits it to do so. (The early preparation of *a* also makes the note played by *i* staccato, so that a uniform clipping of each treble note tells the ear that the mechanical procedure is working.) As the speed of the tremolo increases, the simultaneous preparation of *p* and *a* will split apart; in fact, it must do so for the melody to seem continuous. The value of the simultaneous preparation in slow practice is that at the highest speeds, *a* will still keep a residual sense of security—of "being there ahead of time." The support of the thumb plus the extra time for preparation virtually eliminates the problem of accuracy with the *a* finger.

An aggressive tremolo is sometimes called a "machine-gun" tremolo. The image isn't bad; in fact, to pursue it further leads one to a comparison with the actual mechanism of a toy machine gun. In this, a crank turns the flexible spokes of a little paddle block against a flange. The release of each spoke brings the next sharply down, creating a clacking noise. If the tremolo is practiced for control, then the physical sensations, the underlying mechanics, and the sound produced can be understood in similar terms:

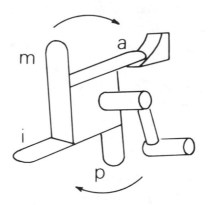

The execution of *a* above will bring *m* immediately into prepared position, ready to play. The execution of *m* will do likewise for *i*, and so on. In each case, the preceding note is cut short with a distinct click by the seating of a nail.

This control of articulation must be learned and practiced at a snail's pace. The fact that it is a practice strategy, not a performance technique, should always be kept in mind. The first beat (not measure!) of "Recuerdos de la Alhambra," for example, can be written as it should sound in this format:

As the player's command of this articulation improves, speed should be increased. The effect will now be more or less as shown below:

In the above example, the tremolo is played at two-thirds speed. Faster than that the sense of individual finger preparation becomes less and less distinct. We become more aware of the movement as a cycle, and we begin to hear the melody. Finally, with no change in the character of touch the staccato effect simply disappears for all practical purposes. What remains is a fluent tremolo effect, at tempi from ♩ = 138 and higher. The tremolo, indeed, illustrates strikingly how slow staccato practice promotes the effect of legato at performance tempi.

As clear enunciation of consonants is necessary for effective speech, so is clear articulation for musical "pronunciation." This is obvious enough in the case of an instrument such as the violin, where so many articulations from a pointed staccato to a singing legato are possible. But it is just as true in a different way of the guitar, because here the clear detaching of notes happens to be inseparable from solid tone production, from accuracy, and from velocity.

Clear articulation also lies at the threshold of instrumental artistry. Few listeners are aware that what they perceive as a flowing, sparkling performance is the outcome of more or less continuous effort to shape, focus, delay, rush, lengthen or abbreviate the consecutive tones of a piece. This kind of note modeling presumes the use of the prepared attack. The systematic practice of staccato articulation is thus a way of accustoming oneself to the physical and musical prerequisites of the most expressive playing.

When so plain a weakness of the guitar is its inability to sustain, the advocacy of a deliberately staccato touch may seem paradoxical. Always keep in mind, though that: (1) the staccato effect comes from the attempt to prepare notes, not cut them short; (2) it is primarily a practice technique; and (3) it can be controlled at will. The development of right-hand technique is synonymous with the progressive lessening of the time needed to prepare notes effectively. The more time between preparation and execution, the more control. As the "dead space" between notes is lessened the articulation becomes less pronounced. What remains ultimately is an impression of legato, derived from the equal intensity and rhythmic exactitude with which notes are formed and placed.

CHAPTER SIX

Coordination and Velocity

The full value of right-hand preparations becomes apparent when we use them to coordinate the hands. Accurate playing at high speeds demands this coordination. As tempo or subdivision of beat increases, conscious control decreases and reflexes take over. This is where correct practice pays off, for the reasons suggested by Ortmann:

> By repetition of voluntary movement, which must always begin under direct brain control, the brain is needed less and less until finally it is relieved of all participation and we have what is known as an acquired reflex, the work of the spinal centers. . . . The value of repetition and drill is to transfer the neural representation of a movement from the higher brain centers to the lower spinal reflex centers.[1]

In turn, we must understand in detail, and with the clarity of a slow-motion film, the nature and timing of those movements. Once understood, they can be instilled as reflexes through repetition at gradually increasing velocities.

In essence, coordination is the overlapping of the left-hand *movement* impulse by the right-hand *preparation* impulse. As a general rule, "the right hand anticipates the left" describes the feel of coordinated movement. The "small silence" thereby created in Leopold Mozart's phrase has several advantages, some of which have already been discussed. Two more may be mentioned here: (1) the left hand moves with more freedom upon strings which are damped momentarily by the right hand, and (2) the damping effect prevents extraneous string noise in the left hand.

SCALES

In practicing scales, try to develop a wide-angle vision of the action of both hands by looking at your knee or at the floor. Let the thumb rest on a bass string for right-hand support. Coordinate the preparation of the right-hand finger with the attack of the left-hand finger, and note the simultaneity of the tactile sensations coming from the tips. Then, and only then, execute the note with the right hand and repeat the procedure for the next note. Impulses are synchronized accordingly:

Impulse 1:

Right hand prepares
Left hand finds note

Impulse 2:

Right hand executes

Any deviation from this sequence will confuse the clarity of the pattern by splitting the first impulse. The consequent "flutter" between impulses hastens the breakdown of accuracy at high speeds, where the movements of the hands can no longer be consciously coordinated. The faster you can deliberately articulate in practice, the more reliable will be your scales at peak velocity.

For a practice model take a simple chromatic movement along the E string in first position played very slowly:

Now, as you play this, try to cut each note to a fraction of its written value by a quick preparation of each right-hand finger: *i* plays, *m* quickly prepares; *m* plays, *i* quickly prepares, and so on. Each preparation should lock the nail against the string, with flesh contact from above only. Musically, the effect will be as follows:

To continue this movement up the string to the octave requires two position shifts. Compare the versions of shift below (shift point marked by a wedge):

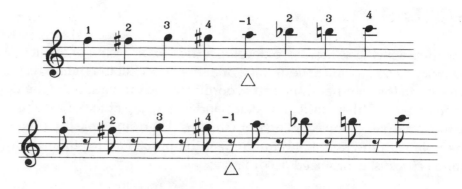

In the first version, a futile effort at legato demands a sudden movement of the left hand at the last possible instant. In the second, the right hand helps the left to find a rhythmically more natural timing by masking the shift with an articulation pause. The shared impulse of the two hands (right hand, prepare; left hand, shift) helps connect the notes so that they seem physically less disjunct, while the deadening of the string prevents extraneous sound. The same technique applies to *all* shifts in *all* scales.

The value of this technique becomes quite critical in consecutive descending shifts, because these will tend to "freeze" the arm. The descending chromatic scale along a single string is an example. We have already considered this scale as an exercise in left-hand control (chapter 2, p. 24). Now let us look at it again as an exercise in coordination. (The scale is given this time on the entire length of the second string):

Played without articulation the rhythm of the scale will fragment into groups marked by the shift points. The shifts themselves will be heard distinctly by changes in accent. It is possible to play this scale so that a listener cannot hear the shifts if a staccato treatment is used and the left hand retains immaculate position during the shifts. Practice slowly enough so that the left hand can shift with no sense of hurry. Establish a base of perfect competence; then increase the tempo and lessen the staccato bite. The point, of course, is not to play perfect one-string chromatics, but to synchronize the hands. Once the principle of timing is felt in the hands, it can be applied in more elaborate contexts and with less conscious emphasis on preparation.

String changes require a subtle change in right-hand finger position, a larger movement, and just a bit more time than notes on the same string. This is particularly so in (1) "cross-fingerings," where an ascending string change is made by the *i* finger, or a descending string change by the *m* finger; and (2) descending string change generally, because the finger must work against gravity and must contract further to find its target. At points of string change, then, decisive preparation is especially important. (It helps also to begin a scale or scale passage on the finger which will produce the least number of cross-fingerings.)

As we move from the first to the sixth string during a scale, there must be also some change in the position of the right arm. Of the three possibilities—contraction of the (1) wrist, (2) forearm, and (3) upper arm—a combination of (2) and (3) is best. Contraction at the wrist produces excessive arch when playing the lower strings, and this is detrimental to velocity (see below). Contraction of the forearm alone results in an angular path across the strings from right to left, with a resulting loss in color-consistency from treble to bass. This movement also tends to be somewhat cramped. Movement of the upper arm from the shoulder combined with some forearm play permits the greatest freedom, accuracy, and control of tone. The movement resembles the action of the bow arm for the cello, though of course it is smaller than that. Thus, the elbow moves to the rear during the course of a descending scale, forward during an ascending scale. Naturally, the forearm must rest lightly enough to be able to slide back and forth freely (see also chapter 1, p. 11).

The supported thumb also helps make string changing more secure. Many players keep the thumb on the sixth string throughout a scale. Others (Segovia included) use it as a shifting point of support two or three strings below the treble string being played. One or the other is necessary. The player should experiment to determine personal preference.

The basic two-octave C major scale played for coordination effect will sound as follows:

Notice the occasional quarter notes. They occur at string changes, are approximate values only, and indicate that in ascending, lower string notes will continue to ring; in descending, higher string notes will continue to ring. Do not try to shorten the quarter notes until the coordination scheme has been mastered. When it has been, you can introduce the following refinements to make all notes equal in length:

1. In ascending, let the right-hand finger lean back as part of its preparatory movement to stop the lower string with flesh contact.

2. In descending, let the left-hand finger lean back in making its new note to stop the higher string with a similar flesh contact.

Though seemingly extraneous, these movements are quite natural. The mind accepts them as part of the preparation impulse. Thus absorbed by habit, they soon become an ear-regulated aspect of technique.

The rewards of articulated scale practice are various. Especially important are the improvements in rhythmic finesse and evenness of attack. There is, for example, a nearly universal tendency to accent unevenly the subdivisions of a beat. This tendency usually works against the sense of phrase in all but short rhythmic motifs. Staccato practice will help correct it by promoting equal stress of all notes (see also chapter 8, p. 112). Another important consequence of this sort of practice is increased right-hand facility because of the shorter movements and more precise nail use that staccato practice encourages. The left hand benefits too, because of the masking of shift points by articulations.The more frequent or more difficult the shifts, the more evident the value for the left hand of this coordination principle.

VELOCITY IN SCALES

As a coordination and velocity exercise, practicing the Segovia scales (see Bibliography) is still unsurpassed. The scales should be played always in distinct rhythmic groupings—eighths, triplets, and sixteenths:

never just as an unmeasured, unaccented succession of notes. Remember also that for two-octave scales in triplets and three-octave scales in sixteenths an "extra" note (preferably the leading-tone beneath the lowest tonic) must be added in order to keep the accentuation symmetrical in repeats. Use both the *i-m* and *m-a* alternations; the latter is one of the very best ways to strengthen the *a* finger. The *a-m-i* alternation also strengthens the *a* finger and improves the overall balance of the touch. Alternation of the stronger *i-m* pair is the most reliable way to play fast passages, however. A virtuoso performer can handle all the Segovia scales in sixteenths at $\quarternote = 144$ and faster with this touch. A respectable speed for most serious guitarists would be $\quarternote = 132$ in sixteenths.

Make a distinction between *controlled speed* and *raw speed*. The former is the speed at which deliberate articulation is still possible, the latter that at which it is not. Past a point it is impossible to increase raw speed voluntarily, but as controlled speed increases, so does raw speed. Determine with the metronome the fastest speed at which you can play a given scale and record the figure. Determine next your best controlled speed figure. It may be only half the raw speed figure at the outset. That doesn't matter. As you become more accustomed to preparation, your controlled speed will increase—and with it your raw speed.

Keep written records of your progress. Time and again tape recordings of one's playing will prove that what sounded fast was sluggish, while something else that seemed to drag was in fact quite lively. The development of an accurate sense of tempo may take years. It is a part of musicianship that should develop together with technique, and one way to see that it does is to make frequent objective reference to the metronome. Like the mechanical rabbit at the dog races, the metronome also serves as a necessary incentive when practicing for velocity.

A diary of speeds attained during a month in which you concentrate on this type of development can be very reassuring. Ten-percent improvement is common. Over a year or more, staccato scale practice can improve one's speed by half. Increases of more than 30 percent, for example from sixteenth notes at ♩ = 92 to ♩ = 126, are typical.

When one has reached a fairly fluent level of velocity (for instance, the three-octave E, F, or G major scale at ♩ = 120 in sixteenths), it is usually necessary to lighten the touch to progress further. The really sparkling execution of scales depends upon a light touch in both hands. At virtuoso speed levels, tone is secondary. Economy of movement, on the other hand, is paramount.

The reason for this is clear enough if you think of the alternation of fingers as resembling somewhat the back-and-forth movements of a pendulum. Make a common ring-on-a-string pendulum; swing it back and forth, and note how each movement is "braked" by the cessation of its own momentum. A comparable sense of equilibrium in the fingers requires tiny relaxations at the end of each half of the stroke: flexor, relax/extensor, contract; extensor, relax/flexor, contract; thus each muscle can operate unimpeded by the other. As velocity increases, however, so does the extent of the muscular contractions, and together with that, the momentum of the fingers. Furthermore, the amount of time in which the relaxation can occur lessens almost to zero. The result is that the weak extensor must literally fight the flexor in order to return the finger to a usable position. The greater exertion results in a larger recovery, thereby uselessly widening the stroke. Past a certain point, there will be no increase in speed for much the same reason that no matter how violently you swing your string pendulum, you cannot make it move any faster past a certain point. Cannot, that is, without shortening the string. As you shorten the string more and more, the ring will move back and forth progressively faster without any greater effort on your part. And for much the same reason, if you shorten your stroke it will be faster too.

Since we are dealing here with such minute distances, it is best to approach the stroke-shortening process from the standpoint of physical sensations rather than micro-measurements. Some control of extensor action is already built into the process of stroke preparation. Preparatory movements restrict the recovery and incorporate it within the physical sensation of the attack. There is little more that can be done to shorten the recovery directly. Extensor movements, however, tend to balance flexor movements with an equivalent force. The more energetic your attack, the more energetic your recovery is likely to be. Conversely, as you restrain the intensity of attack, you shorten the recovery.

The attempt merely to play softer may help. Overplaying is a common cause of sluggishness in otherwise very well-developed players. The reason is that speed and volume are inversely related. Past a point, if you want to play faster, you must also play with less intensity. The principle applies throughout the range of technique, not only to scales, and for that matter, not only to the guitar. But underplaying has drawbacks too, such as weak tone and rhythmic slackness; it is also fairly common among intermediate to advanced guitarists. Therefore, if we want a lighter touch in scales without sacrifice of incisiveness, we will need to employ some specific practice techniques for that purpose. The following will help increase your scale velocity to virtuoso levels:

1. Lower the wrist and curl the fingers more than you would for ordinary playing. This puts the fingertips directly on a line of force with the playing muscles in the forearm. It also lessens the bite of the nails, making for less string resistance:

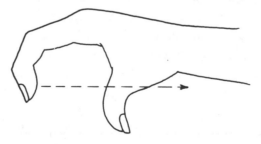

Rest strokes performed from this position feel decidedly different from rest strokes performed from a higher wrist position. The muscular exertion seems confined to the palm of the hand, and although this is an illusion fostered by the mechanical efficiency of the position, the sensation of lessened muscular effort is certainly real enough. (The tendency of the elbow to move outward and the shoulder to roll forward when lowering the wrist is natural and shouldn't be inhibited.)

2. Keep the tip-joints absolutely firm. Any joint collapse, no matter how small, can only slow the stroke. (Experimentation with the piano has

shown that the collapse of a joint increases the time required for key-depression by more than 100 percent, from 2/50 to 5/50 of a second.)[2] In fact, it may help even to think of the stroke as originating in an actual flex of the fingertip, as if scratching a mosquito bite.

3. Restrain the attack in extremely slow practice by trying to stop the finger short of the string it comes to rest against. Of course, this is next to impossible, but the effort to "brake" the stroke this way will, when unconscious reflex takes over, lighten it further without sacrificing incisiveness. The recovery will seem to be an instantaneous short recoil, like the pounce of a cat's paw. Strokes performed in this manner are more akin to free stroke than to the weightier kind of rest stroke used in slower playing or for emphasis. They also help to promote indirectly the light left hand touch so necessary for fluent playing (p. 32).

CHORDS

Chords may not at first glance seem to present the technical problems of scales, but there are exceptions. Besides, there is a basic difference in musical effect between chords that are well articulated and chords that are not. The difference lies not only in the more accurate rhythm of the former but also in the clarity afforded by clean endings and the suppression of extramusical sounds.

Numerous pieces require a deliberate articulation of chords. The Sor Estudio 9 (quoted on page 25) is the perfect textbook case, but other less obvious examples abound. All six of the Milan Pavans, the Roncalli Passacaglia, Dowland's "Queen Elizabeth Galliard," Tansman's "Danza Pomposa," Rodrigo's "Sarabanda Lejana," and many, many more are built around sequences of short chords for which distinct and rhythmic articulation is stylistically appropriate. And beyond this, there are chordal pieces of a more legato nature which nonetheless profit enormously from staccato practice.

The rule for right-hand, left-hand coordination in chord playing is simply that the right hand anticipates the left. The right-hand fingers should block out their positions for the next chord before the left hand leaves the position which it is holding. Consider playing this cadential figure:

The preparation pattern would be as follows (*x*'s indicate string placement of right-hand fingers):

Notes are shortened to approximately half their value by the decisive preparation; later on, a more delicate preparation that shortens them much less will be enough. In this comfortable space of silence, the left hand can move freely, timing the beginning of each movement by the right hand's preparation so that the hands are synchronized by a common impulse. The physical grace and musical clarity of chord changes upon strings that have been deadened momentarily by the right hand are immediately apparent and may come as a pleasant surprise.

Note that the highest voice will continue to ring when blocking for the A minor and G major chords; the bass will ring when blocking for the F and the final C. As in the case of scales, make no attempt to silence such notes when learning the technique. The left hand can generally find ways to equalize treble note values by flattening a finger when necessary. The same will often work for bass notes. In the case of overlapping open basses, a separate gesture of the thumb after the chord change is usually the best way to silence the unwanted tone:

Here again, the technique succeeds by virtue of a small deception: the ear accepts the silencing of the E as simultaneous with the execution of A, although in fact there is a small overlap. (The alternative procedure of sandwiching the thumb between the strings to silence the E with the back of the thumb is less satisfactory, even though sometimes the only way.)

As in the case of scales, preparation becomes really indispensable when more awkward left-hand movements are involved. Often experience shows what may seem at first a left-hand problem to be really a coordination problem. The shift in measures 11-12 in the Albéniz "Granada" is a fair example.

The shift should be taken with the most convincing impression of legato the player can summon since the second measure merely prolongs the melody note B in the bass. Unfortunately, the shift is awkward. The use of correct elbow anticipation discussed in chapter 2 will help, but it will not entirely solve the problem of how to smooth over the little ragged edges of sound.

The solution is, just as in scale playing, to mask the shift with an articulation (indicated by the x's). The right-hand fingers clamp down for the new formation before the left hand begins to move, allowing it to move on deadened strings with consequently greater clarity. The value of this technique to enhance the effect of legato in shifting is demonstrated time and again. There is a marked similarity here to the timing of bow change for shifts in cello technique:

> A position change takes a certain amount of time even if it is executed very quickly. We must be aware of this time, since it normally has no rhythmic value of its own. . . . The position change must be considered as a pickup; it must occur before the rhythmic stress of the new tone....The bow is changed before the rhythmic stress....and will produce a soft "consonantal" noise before the new tone.[3]

On both cello and guitar, this "soft consonantal noise" functions as a minute rhythmic silence introduced by the right hand to cover the movement of the left. Since it is absorbed into the rhythmic structure as a kind of upbeat to the next stress, it is not objectionable, even if quite pronounced. In the Albéniz example above and many others like it, once the real timing of the shift is mastered, the articulation will become progressively more subconscious. As it does, less time will be needed to prepare the chord. Eventually the shift will seem to come with legato fluency.

There is even a parallel with a technique employed in woodwind playing to smooth over rough spots with deliberate articulation:

> In its simplest form, *legato* means a connection between notes in which the breath does not stop . . . . In actual practice, however, there is usually some time taken between the notes during which

the new settings are prepared. The more time this takes, the less smooth this connection will be . . . . The bigger the skip the more difficult. This particular problem can sometimes be overcome by using the tongue in a very discreet way. If this is done properly it is hard to tell that the tongue has been used. . . . Even though it is not heard, it has the effect of breaking the air column and making the problem note speak more easily.[4]

What is involved here would seem a common musical problem; namely, how to fit the normal rhythmic stress around some technical difficulty, such as a large intervalic skip. Not surprisingly, therefore, does the solution involve a related principle of timing and mechanics even in the case of instruments which are unrelated in technique.

Pursuing the woodwind analogy one step further, it may help to think of taking a short "breath" before difficult shifts. But even when the shifts are not particularly awkward, the use of right-hand preparations will make the left hand more fluent. Tiny relaxations are possible within the general limits of left-hand discipline when the hand is spared from hugging the strings until the last possible instant and then jumping abruptly to the new position. Real grace of left-hand movement can only come about through the assistance of the right hand (see also chapter 8, p. 114).

The notorious Estudio 12 by Sor is an outstanding example, particularly measures 5 through 7. Seldom does one hear this passage played without error in live performance because of the split-second timing and the tendency of the arm muscles to freeze in the consecutive descending movements. The use of preparations permits small but essential relaxations of the left arm during the shifts. This, together with the more accurate timing thereby fostered will make the passage much more playable. (So will the left-hand fingering given here.) Practice with crisp staccato throughout, so that shifts sound no different from notes taken within the same position. (Bass-note values are as in Segovia and Williams recordings):

The wedges above indicate only actual position shift—that is, the movement of the thumb from one place on the neck to another. Observe that in measures 2 and 3, the fingers alternate from fourth to fifth position without disturbing the thumb; it can rotate on its tip to accommodate. Neither is there true position change in measures 4 and 5; the thumb remains essentially in ninth position. This lessens the number of consecutive descending shifts. The player can now focus clearly on the one place where trouble is likely to arise: the shifts in measures 5 and 6. Practice these measures separately, with emphasis on strict finger position and graceful arm movement.

While a markedly détaché rendering is appropriate to many kinds of chordal pieces, it is not to all. The popular Bach chorale arrangements by Christopher Parkening are cases in point. The silkiest legato possible are what these pieces deserve—and, in Parkening's sensitive handling, get. Nonetheless, practice of such pieces with deliberate right-hand preparation is the surest guarantee of ultimate legato fluency in performance. The point applies to numerous pieces in the standard repertoire: Prelude 6 by Ponce, Andante Largo by Sor, and Prelude 5 by Villa-Lobos are but a few.

For arpeggio figures, the same rule as for single-impulse chords applies: block the new position with the right hand before moving the left. The more difficult the shift, the more evident the value of the technique. Even an old chestnut like the "Romance Anonimo" has a few difficulties that can be eliminated by blocking the chord shifts in advance with *p* and *a*:

The same *p-a* anticipation belongs to the tremolo and can be used to advantage repeatedly in "Recuerdos de la Alhambra". No matter what the nature of the cyclical movement, the thumb and at least one other finger can be used to prepare a shift. The procedure soon becomes a reflex action, a subconscious principle of timing that imparts a sense of freedom to the left hand and of accuracy to the right.

HOMOPHONIC AND CONTRAPUNTAL TEXTURES

Most music for the guitar (excepting the large etude literature) consists neither wholly of chords, scales, nor arpeggios, but of various combinations of all three. In the playing of such music, the coordination techniques described previously have their most sophisticated use.

The Granados "Danza Espanola No. 5," although a transcription, is a good example of a musical texture very common in guitar music—broken chords with melody—as in the first five measures quoted below:

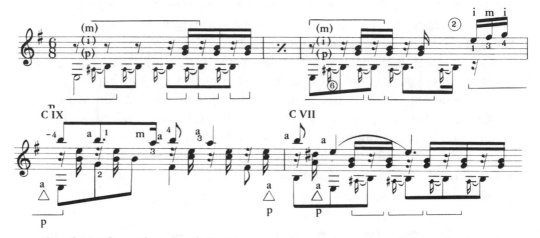

Brackets show that the following preparations are possible in the first three measures:

1. By playing the initial E with a rest stroke, the thumb prepares its subsequent A sharp-B on the fifth string. (Use of the rest stroke to prepare a stroke upon the next higher string in this way is quite common; cf. the Villa-Lobos Etude 1 formula, p. 66 above.)

2. The first *m-i* execution in each measure is prepared at the beginning of the measure simultaneously with *p*. The planting of fingers like this gains security for the thumb and is a natural, beneficial technique. (Any similar form of contact that steadies the hand without inadvertently silencing notes is good.)

3. *P-i-m* can prepare together as for a single chord in order to execute the subsequent impulses of the broken E minor chord.

The end of the third measure introduces the melody. An *i-m-i* sequence is preferable to *m-i-m* because *i* to *a* in measure 4, as in general, is more reliable and more incisive than *m* to *a*. Note that the bracket overlaps measure 4. This indicates a simultaneous attack of *p* and *i* that prepares the initial bass E in the next measure and stops the preceding bass B for a clean melodic entry. Play the three sixteenth notes free stroke, as also the sixteenth note in measure 4; they sound heavy if played rest stroke. In slow practice, give them the staccato articulation usual for the practice of scales; at tempo, there will of course be no deliberate effort to shorten them.

The *a* finger prepares for its first note in measure 4 as for a chord shift. It should be in place before the left hand moves. The same applies to the other two chord changes in the passage (indicated by wedges). The *a* finger plays rest stroke here and throughout in the interest of melodic emphasis.

A handsome reward awaits the guitarist patient enough to study pieces in the above manner. The learning chain begins with the conscious control of movement whose details have been exaggerated for greater clarity. In turn, it becomes enriched with tactile and auditory impressions that the exaggeration renders more vivid so as to engrave them upon the motor areas of the brain. Gradually a reflex arc is established. The movement becomes more automatic and, concomitantly, more fluid, adroit, and relaxed. Eventually, it is ear-regulated and subconscious.[5]

Contrapuntal textures offer the most challenging and rewarding opportunities for this kind of study. Listen to the John Williams recording of the Bach Allegro in D ("More Virtuoso Music for Guitar", Columbia MS 6939). Note the utter cleanliness of the presentation and the crisp articulation which immediately suggests the harpsichord affinities of this work. Not all of us can hope to play the piece with Williams' drive and spirit, but it is not unrealistic for any serious player to try for the same careful modeling of sound. It is simply a matter of anticipating each left-hand movement with the corresponding placement of a right-hand finger. In particular, consider the opportunities indicated by brackets and wedges below:

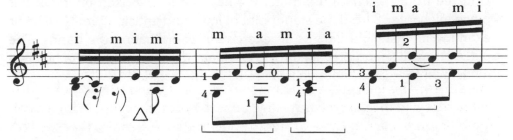

In measures 1 and 2, exactly as in the preceding Granados example, the first bass note prepares simultaneously with the next treble note and, as a rest stroke, prepares the next bass note too. The scalewise descending movement of the bass is outlined clearly by treating it as a series of chord shifts—that is, by blocking each thumb-finger pair of notes before making the left-hand formation. Given the harmonic function of the bass line, it is logical anyway to handle bass-treble note pairs in the manner of chords. In the last two measures, the fingers can be grouped repeatedly as for an ascending arpeggio.

Free stroke is preferable for the treble part in this piece. The same is generally true of rapid contrapuntal textures, both on mechanical and aesthetic grounds. Occasional rest-stroke accents are welcome, but consistent rest stroke is physically awkward (at some points impossible) and comparatively crude-sounding. In the above passage, the initial melodic D is really the only note that calls for rest stroke in the treble. (The thumb may find rest stroke congenial on the first two beats of measure 4, however). One of the specific benefits of practicing this piece and others like it with forced articulation is to improve the free-stroke tone. The articulation gesture encourages that downward push into the string which makes free stroke sound very nearly as full as rest stroke (see above chapter 3, p. 37).

The passage also illustrates another benefit of this kind of study. Note the nonsymmetrical character of the right-hand fingering given—the interpolations of *a* for better finger-to-string correspondence where the melody moves by skip, the shifting of accents from *m* to *i*, the repetition of the *i* finger in measure 2. The fingering given is by no means the only plausible one, but it is practical. Consequently, it incorporates irregularities that simply fall beyond the scope of any arbitrary pattern. The practice of right-hand preparations often helps one find the best fingering for a passage or piece. A kind of hidden logic of the hand will dictate sound finger choice as the outcome of one's efforts to be always on top of the notes. A likely overall result is an increased respect for finger-to-string correspondence, as well as a lessened reliance upon strict alternation patterns. Sometimes it helps also to work backward from a passage whose fingering is obligatory to find the easiest manner of leading into it.

The Allegro in D is a very demanding piece. A more sensible point to begin learning the touch scheme for contrapuntal works would be the Bach Bourrée from the First Lute Suite. We have already looked briefly at this piece in chapter 2 from the standpoint of left-hand anticipation. Now let us examine its first eight bars as an exercise in coordinating the hands. The piece as it will sound practiced for coordination is indicated in the first two measures; thereafter, note values are as in the original:

Eighth notes are bitten off approximately to sixteenths, while quarter notes are allowed the value of dotted eighths. And as a matter of fact, these note values are not abbreviated much more than they should be in actual performance. In the faster Baroque dance tempi, the standard treatment of short notes is always somewhat staccato in the interest of liveliness and point.[6]

The two quarter notes in the bass of measure 1 are occasioned by string change; here, as elsewhere, bass stopping is a refinement that can be introduced later by one of the techniques described earlier in this chapter under "Scales" and "Chords." An *m-i-m* alternation pattern corresponding to the rhythmic figures is the most practical fingering. It is to be played free stroke. (Note the reversal of the pattern for convenience of string change in the third measure). The bass is played free stroke too, but with emphasis; it must speak distinctly if the harmony of the piece is to be heard.

Depending on the tempo and the player's development, the time taken to prepare notes will vary. At the outset, errors in timing are natural. As tempo increases and as the touch becomes more instinctive, the silences between notes will lessen and the notes themselves become less forced in their delivery. Ultimately what will remain is a neat, détaché rendering. It will be natural and relaxed, but it will also be rhythmically aggressive, technically immaculate, and stylistically convincing. Something else will remain too: a transferable coordination pattern which is not only useful for playing baroque music in the proper spirit, but which cuts across the entire repertoire.

Coordination between the hands is achieved by synchronizing the right-hand preparation impulse with the left-hand movement impulse. The rule that "the right hand anticipates the left" generally describes the feeling of coordinated movement. In uncontrolled playing, the right-hand preparatory movement either does not exist at all or is upset by the intensity of the recovery. Systematic staccato practice at gradually increasing tempi develops controlled, economical movement by concentrating upon preparation. The consequent improvement in tone, accuracy, and velocity is directly proportional to the difficulty of the left-hand fingering. In general, a more nimble left hand is one important benefit of the practice of right-hand preparations.

For musical reasons alone, control of articulation is desirable. Various expressive nuances involve small distinctions of loudness, tone color, and rhythm—distinctions which may be meaningless in the absence of a refined, coordinated technique. Given that technique, however, the mastery of expression represents the real challenge and satisfaction of playing the guitar.

CHAPTER SEVEN

Expressive Devices

Several of the expressive possibilities of the guitar should be considered explicit devices as opposed to nuances, the latter of which are the subject of the next chapter. Among these are slurs, vibrato, and a number of right-hand flourishes. A mastery of them imparts polish to performance and helps bridge the gap between the printed score and living music.

SLURS AS ACCENT

We have dealt with slurs in chapter 2 as a form of exercise in finger dexterity. Slurs also are an expressive device common to all strings and woodwinds. While the guitar can never hope to achieve the technical legato implied by ligatures in the music of these other instruments, the relative difference in attack quality of plucked and slurred notes still can be exploited to great effect. An appreciation of the accent value of slurs will help to dispel doubts over when—and when not—to slur.

Slurring from one note to the next results in distinct contrast. First, the plucked note is audibly louder than the slurred note. Furthermore, slurs create a subtle but unmistakeable *agogic* emphasis; plucked notes are not only louder but also a little longer than slurred notes. If the plucked note is played rest stroke, the contrast is greatest. Since slurs emphasize certain notes at the expense of others, their place in melodic phrasing may be likened to that of syllable stress in speech. Some patterns of stress are required for clarity, others for rhetorical effect, and there is scope for individual preference. The choice of when to slur, if at all, is a matter for thought when we are studying a piece. The character of the music, its technical difficulties, the style appropriate to the historical period it represents, the quality of editing—all these must be taken into account.

Slurs presumably came into existence when some player discovered the happy possibility of getting two notes from one right hand effort by plucking or hammering with the left hand. This may well have happened several hundred years ago, on the lute, vihuela, or both. It is sometimes claimed that the double coursing of these instruments makes slurring impractical. The fact remains that the first course of each is a single "chanterelle" string upon which slurs are quite natural. True, an elaborate use of slurs does not suit the character of early music; but slurs should not be excluded merely on historical grounds. Besides, the difference in sonority between the lute or vihuela and the guitar justifies the somewhat more liberal use of slurs on the guitar. Many a passage that would sound monotonous and would be difficult to execute with continuous plucking becomes more colorful and easier to play if discreetly slurred.

The following is a well-known example:

Luis de Narvaez, "Diferencias sobre Guardame las Vacas" (measures 13 - 16)

Regular metric figures gain both in fluency and rhythmic accent, here and in many comparable instances. Here the shifting of metric accent ("hemiola"— a device practically synonymous with Spanish music) is also clarified by slurring strong beats. Note, however, that a slur is not desirable in the next to last measure where the meter seems to call for one (see asterisk). A slur at this point would break the rising line of the phrase by accenting the E and making the F sharp comparatively weak. In general, one should always be careful that the accents imparted by slurs are consistent with the sense of phrase.

A melodic figure frequently expressed well through slurring is the principal note-lower neighbor-principal note formula. The following are some examples of its use as a main motif:

(a)
Bach, Prelude from the First Cello Suite

(b)
Gasper Sanz, "Canarios"

(c) Fernando Sor, Allegro from the "Grand Solo"

(d) Bach, Prelude from Prelude, Fugue, and Allegro

In (a), (b), and (c), slurs are not only justified, they are necessary, and appear in all editions of these pieces. In the case of (d), both the slower tempo and the more elaborate melodic construction call for the lower neighbor to be stressed somewhat more than in the other cases. In fact, it is entirely plausible to treat the lower neighbor here as an accented upbeat to the second principal note. Consequently, the use of a slur here, while optional, is also rather doubtful. Again, slurs that do not enhance the sense of phrase should not be used.

Slurs do not always have to be metric in emphasis, either. They can even go against the beat, as in the following examples from the Allemande from the First Lute Suite by Bach:

Melodic entries frequently justify this kind of syncopated slurring. So do, sometimes, those changes in melodic direction or contour which amount to "hidden" entries:

(Bach, Prelude from Third Cello Suite)

Here and elsewhere it is a good idea to underscore similar motivic material with as nearly identical slur patterns as you can.

Musically valid slurring always enhances either fluency, rhythmic accent, or melodic contour, sometimes all at the same time. By contrast, slurs that detract from any of these should not be used, even if they are written in the score. Editorial overslurring is not as common today as in the past, but one should watch for it, especially in the older Bach editions. Since more than one "correct" slurring is usually possible, responsibility rests with the player to adopt a fingering consistent with his own most deeply felt musical concept of a piece.

VIBRATO

Vibrato is a way of enriching notes by means of rapid fluctuation in pitch (generally accompanied by some secondary fluctuation in intensity). Vibrato of the voice, or "tremolo", seems to be an innate expressive device. Appearing in several unrelated musical cultures, its origins may lie in the tendency of the emotionally charged voice to quiver. In any case, it is so much a part of fine singing as we know it that vibratoless song today is inconceivable. By analogy, all instruments capable of producing vibrato have used it for centuries. The use of string vibrato as an ornament apparently was common in baroque times, and was no novelty then.

There is some controversy today, however, as to whether continual vibrato suits a historically correct style of playing old music. The issue would seem to belong as much to the realm of musical taste as music history. On the one hand, some evidence does exist for the use of a subdued continual string vibrato in the eighteenth century.[1] On the other, objections to the "sempre vibrato" are not confined to the performance of renaissance or baroque music.[2] One likely reason for the controversy is that sensitivity to minute amounts of pitch fluctuation varies even among trained musicians; a vibrato that sounds rich to one listener may possibly offend a more acute ear. Another lies in the appropriateness of the pitch fluctuation to the music at hand, whatever its century. Electronic measurements of the amplitude of pitch fluctuation have shown the average in violin vibrato to be a quarter of a tone. The average among operatic singers is a semitone with some as much as three-quarters of a tone.[3]

A vocal vibrato that does splendidly in the climax of an operatic aria will obviously not suit the performance of a Renaissance madrigal. This does not mean, however, that a perfectly neutral delivery in all early music is desirable, even in the interest of historically "correct" performance. Rather, the intensity should suit the music. The same is true for the guitar. No guitarist should hesitate to use vibrato, but there must be musical taste and good sense in its use. With few exceptions, if the listener is actually aware of vibrato, then there is too much.

Although the vibrato produced on the guitar is similar in effect to that of a violin, the mechanism differs slightly. On bowed instruments, vibrato is commonly produced by the rotation of the fingertip from one side to another, thereby alternately shortening and lengthening the stopped portion of the string by about one-eighth of a tone. On the guitar, the finger by the friction of its pressure literally stretches the string in alternate directions. This causes both increase and decrease in pitch from the mean tone. The amplitude of the pitch fluctuation ranges from less than a quarter tone on the lower frets of the first string, to a potential of more than a semitone on the higher frets of the sixth.

You can test the principle easily. Make the note D at the tenth fret of the sixth string; place the finger in the center of the fret space, midway between the actual ninth and tenth frets. Press hard and push your finger down until it touches the tenth fret. Note the decrease in pitch as you stretch the string away from the nut, thereby slackening the stopped portion. Still pressing hard, pull the finger in the opposite direction until it touches the ninth fret. Note this time the increase in pitch as you increase the tension on the stopped portion of the string. If you repeat these movements alternately you should notice a total pitch fluctuation of about a semitone.

The entire arm is used to produce vibrato on the guitar. Lateral movements of the forearm in rapid succession are resolved against the friction of the fingertip. These movements are practically without muscular effort. They originate in upper arm rotation, but once started, continue of their own momentum exactly like a seesaw or pendulum. In fact, the upper arm and hand do form a kind of seesaw, whose pivotal axis is a point some two or three inches from the elbow:[4]

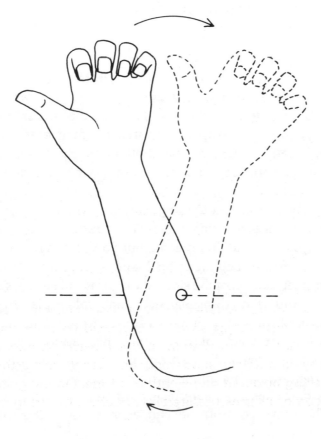

When one shakes a bottle to agitate the contents (mixing frozen orange juice, for example), one performs just such a motion. The seesaw play between hand and elbow is identical for the vibrato. Since the distance traversed by the hand in an actual vibrato is so small, however—perhaps an inch—then there is no perceptible displacement of the elbow. The movement will seem rather to originate in a back-and-forth throw of the hand in which the elbow is the pivot.

You can learn the "feel" of vibrato, without the guitar, in the following way. Place your right forearm across your body so as to simulate the fingerboard; then grasp your right wrist with thumb and second finger, as if holding down a note:

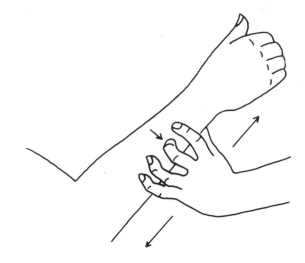

Now shake your left hand back and forth so that it stretches the skin on your right wrist and forearm in alternate directions. Do this rapidly but not spasmodically. Be sure to keep the wrist fixed, so that the hand makes no independent movement. Keep up an even shaking for at least ten seconds. If the movement is free enough, you will notice the muscles in your upper arm jiggling loosely. Your second finger may also wobble slightly from side to side but without losing its grip.

To transfer the movement to the guitar, play the note B on the fourth string at the ninth fret; fourth-string notes in the upper positions are the most responsive. Use your second finger again but do *not* grip the neck with the thumb. The thumb may rest lightly upon the neck, but without pressure. Try to re-create the essential feel of the simulation; above all, make sure that the shaking of the hand is rhythmically even and takes place only in the longitudinal plane of the string. Students sometimes fall into a spasmodic, lateral back-and-forth pushing of the finger. If this happens, go back to the simulation in order to check the appropriate sensations; repeat until you can do the movement on the guitar without strain.

All good vibrato has a regular pulse; poor vibrato is nervous-sounding and erratic. The more control you can exercise over the rate of pitch fluctuation, the more spontaneous and natural your vibrato will be in performance. A good test, and exercise in control, is to sustain a continuous vibrato on the fourth-string B slowly enough to count regular pulsations:

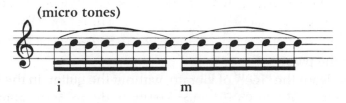

Some experimenting will show that different intensities of vibration are necessary for different strings and fingerboard positions. Take the following three notes as an example:

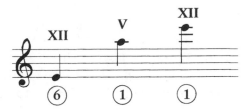

A vibrato appropriate for the sixth string E will not produce audible pitch fluctuation on the first-string A. Conversely, the same intensity that makes a nice vibrato on the A will make the sixth string E sound grotesque. The intensity appropriate to the first string E falls between these extremes. Broadly speaking, therefore, in moving from bass strings to treble, or from higher to lower on the same string, the intensity of vibrato must increase.

One does not have to create a flurry of sound for the vibrato to add life and color. Even two or three vibrations on a few notes can make the difference between wooden playing and music that sings. The beginning of Tárrega's "Lagrima" offers as plain and simple an example as can be found:

The rising melodic line can be dramatized nicely while retaining the simple charm of the music by a restrained vibrato on A and B. Two vibrations will do for A; three or four for B will emphasize its climactic value. The F-sharp coming at the end of the phrase does not need the emphasis that vibrato imparts. But what if it did? The strings are so stiff at lower frets that vibrato by the usual means is inefficient. In those cases where vibrato at a fret below the fourth really seems desirable, another technique is used: the lateral-bend vibrato. In this form of vibrato the finger, flexing from its tip and middle joints, moves the string from side to side.

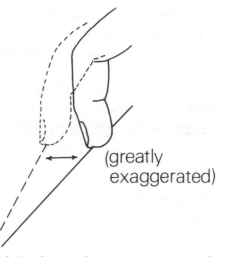

(greatly exaggerated)

The shortcomings of this form of vibrato are several. First, since it can only increase the tension on the string, the pitch fluctuation consists entirely in a sharping of the mean tone. Second, it is harder to control and tends to be obtrusive. Third, it is less natural than the normal vibrato and cannot be done with quite the same careless ease.

Its virtues, however, make its mastery eminently worthwhile; these include its use in the lower positions. Normal vibrato in the very highest register is also impractical because of the quick decay of the notes and the narrowness of the frets. To make the highest A or B speak clearly, a lateral bend vibrato is necessary. Again, a very few vibrations will suffice; if the movement is done properly, the note will actually seem to swell.

Finally, this type of vibrato can be used to dramatize single notes in chords without making the entire chord quaver. Try making the lowest note of the inverted C major seventh below and the highest note of the following G major vibrate without disturbing the other fingers in either chord:

The first can be found, among other places, at the end of Torroba's "Preambulo" (No. 1 of *Piéces Characteristiques*) and profits there from this nuanced handling of the dissonant bass. A pointed example of the second is in Sor's Estudio 17, measure 13 (quoted above, p. 25) where the melody can be made to sing with this technique.

RIGHT-HAND FLOURISHES

In most playing the technical requirements of the music call for a fairly strict right-hand position. So much is this so that a master player can create a variety of tone color with a hand that seems hardly to move (see chapter 8). There are exceptions, however.

One is when the heel of the hand rests on the bridge to mute the strings for a pizzicato-effect (sometimes also termed *étouffé* or *apagado*). Just over the saddle is the best place for the flesh contact to occur; if too much of the string is muted, the note will not speak. The fleshy side of the thumb played rest stroke generally produces the best sound, although nail tone can sometimes be interesting. A kind of pizzicato color can even be had from playing with the fleshy side without resting the heel of the hand on the bridge.

Another exception is the tambor, a kettledrum effect involving a percussive blow of the thumb upon the strings immediately in front of the bridge. This rare but colorful effect (usually indicated as "tam." or "percussion") is prepared by resting the little finger just back of the bridge, and then bringing the thumb down smartly with a quick rotation of the forearm, pivoting at the elbow.

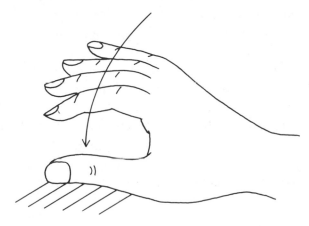

The hand makes no independent movement, and should recoil from the strings with a little bounce. An interesting "edge" to the sound can be provided by the back of the thumbnail. This is especially useful when the first string should be heard clearly, as in Turina's "Fandanguillo," measures 88–92.

A third exception is the manner in which chords are played. Whether in succession in a chordal piece, at cadential points, as punctuation, or as endings, chords afford the opportunity for a broad range of flourishes. Probably the most common of these is the "rolled" or broken chord.

The arpeggiation of chords is one of the most charming guitaristic effects; it is also one of the most abused. When an insensitive or careless player uses it crudely and without relief, it is intolerable. There is no major player who does not arpeggiate quite freely, but as in the case of vibrato, effective use of the technique presumes a certain musical discretion.

Basically, arpeggiation is a device to enrich texture or sonority. The separation of notes in time is accepted by the ear as the equivalent of separation in musical space. The wide spacing of parts possible on the piano renders arpeggiation generally superfluous. Not so the guitar. Its narrower compass and smaller sonority welcome the frequent use of arpeggiations not only for harplike chords but also for the separation of voices in polyphonic textures. Note, for example, in the first measures of Dowland's "Lachrimae Pavan" how the rising line of the interior voice is clarified by separation:

The problems arise when chords are spread too broadly, making them rhythmically vague. Also, if the thumb plays on the beat, the upper notes must necessarily come after the beat. When the highest note is melodic (as it usually is), the result is a delayed stress—perhaps appropriate if the intended effect is rubato or espressivo, but more often simply inept-sounding.

The solution, however, is not necessarily to limit arpeggiation to a special, occasional "effect." It is possible to separate the notes so slightly that the arpeggiation is scarcely heard. It is also possible to begin the chord before the beat so as to place the highest note on the beat. This is how most broken chords should in fact be played—each arpeggiation in the Dowland above, for example. Rhythmically, lower notes have the effect of grace notes:

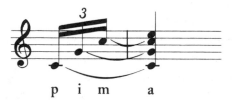

Chords played this way can sound more rhythmic than if played "straight." A dramatic example can be seen at the beginning of the second variation of the Aria con Variazoni ("La Frescobalda") by Frescobaldi:

If the arpeggiated chord of emphasis in each case is begun well before the beat so the highest note falls exactly on the beat, the effect is magnificent.

Both chords, by the way, sound well when played with a sweep of the thumb. Execution of the thumb sweep is best understood as a series of rest strokes, with the thumb literally falling into each successive string. Present the full fleshy side of the tip for best effect; open the hand and push downward from the elbow. There should be no wrist movement and the thumb should bump its way over the strings in a strict perpendicular plane. Emphasize the first string with a small outward turn:

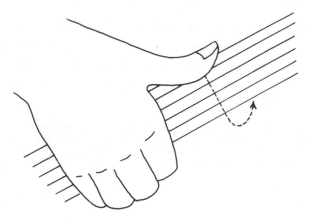

(Note that this stroke is different from the nail sweep, which is done from the wrist, is less sonorous, and is used rather sparingly because of its harsh effect.)

Broken chords played with thumb and fingers differ somewhat from the *p-i-m-a* arpeggio to which they are related. Whereas the fingertips must be firm for the arpeggio, they should be rather flexible for the broken chord. Make no attempt to articulate the notes separately; all the notes of a broken chord are produced by one impulse of a hand prepared as if to play a single solid chord. The natural emphasis is on the highest note, and although the lowest note can also be made to stand out, all others are respectively subordinate. In a broken chord of more than four notes the thumb plays the lowest two or three by a continuous rest stroke—similar to the full thumb sweep, except that here the nail is used. Depending upon whether the thumb plays one, two, or three strings, the natural rhythm of a broken chord will be as follows:

The best way to practice these arpeggiations is by deliberately emphasizing their rhythm. Begin by spacing the notes widely; gradually close them up while keeping the even spacing and the rhythmic accent. Be careful when the thumb plays more than one note to keep the spacing even and to play with consistent nail tone.

In the last measure, the sound should be a "whisk"—a blur of notes not audibly separate in time from the emphatic highest note. In achieving this effect it helps to "throw" the hand to the left, as if flicking lint off one's coat. This lessens nail resistance and quickens the succession of notes (see also chapter 8, p. 109).

A logical practice form for the thumb sweep similarly emphasizes the rhythm in progressively faster executions. Play continuous ascending rest stroke, bumping the fleshy side of the tip over each string with identical emphasis:

Keep the stroke perpendicular to the strings. When mastered, it is best done with flair and an outward flourish of the hand.

GRACE, EMPHASIS, CLOSURE

Like the thumb sweep above, many expressive effects require specific arm or hand movements. Appropriate gestures also help dramatize the music—for yourself, for other players in an ensemble, or for an audience. There are several gestures that are commonly employed in expressive performance.

Energetic chords at points of emphasis (such as the cadential A minor in the Narvaez example, p. 88) can be given proper stress by a whiplash follow-through. The hand moves down and to the right, and with a snap of the wrist returns to its position above the strings. It describes a tight outward circle in so doing. The greater energy of the chord pluck itself will tend to close the hand into a fist:

If the chord comes at a really big cadence, then a more expansive version of this gesture is effective. It will take the upper arm momentarily away from the guitar, and its arc will bring the hand to a position of repose above the strings and back of the sound hole.

When a closing chord must be stopped quickly, the worst way to do so is by laying the open palm over the strings. This inept gesture will blur the ending and imply timidity to an audience. There are several better ways of which the following are a few. If a finger of the left hand is free (as for the common A or E chord), it can clamp down at the moment the right hand snaps into the final position of the illustration above. If no left-hand finger is free, the heel of the right hand can be used, with a quick outward rotation of the forearm. When accompanied by a quick release of the left hand that brings the hand to rest against the upper bout, this is a graceful form of sudden closure. The two hands move decisively toward each other; in silencing they also fall into a neat posture of repose:

When by contrast the sound should ring on, then still other movements will increase duration and sonority. A repeated sequence of gentle chords, such as in the Estudio 1 by Sor:

is enhanced by a bobbing motion from the wrist. This lessens the sense of string resistance, balances the plucking action by a gesture of repose, and frames the movement cycle within an airy, dancelike form:

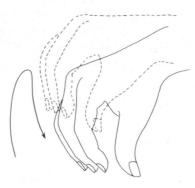

When chords are of longer duration, a large outward circle of the hand will seem literally to draw forth the sound from the instrument:

Frequently a prolonged chord can be given a small, neat closure by a combination of this gesture together with the stopping action of a free left-hand finger. At the last moment, make a small, quick circle with the right hand (the dotted line above the strings) to "cover" the left hand stop. The movement will finish the sound like the flick of a conductor's baton.

If gestures such as those described above seem theatrical, remember that the performance of music is a theatrical art. Overcoming inhibition is necessary for effective performance. Do not hesitate to use gestures that will help you dramatize the music—and yourself.

RASGUEADO

The technique of playing chords with the back of the fingernails is time-honored. A basic distinction between *rasgueado* ("strummed") and *punteado* ("plucked") was recognized in sixteenth-century Spain for the vihuela. The baroque guitar of Corbetta, deVisee, and Roncalli made regular use of up-and-down-strokes of the first finger. More recently, modern composers such as Rodrigo, Turina, John Duarte, Manual Ponce, and Lennox Berkeley have employed rasgueado in their compositions for its coloristic effect. In so doing, they have been influenced not so much by the historical use of rasgueado in classical playing as by its more striking use in flamenco music. The work of guitar composers of all nationalities reflects the powerful appeal of the folkloric Spanish guitar. It is to the techniques of flamenco, therefore, that the informed classical player will logically turn in learning to perform rasgueado properly.

The simplest rasgueado is one in which the four fingers brush lightly across the strings in the sequence *c-a-m-i*, with no particular attempt at separation.[5] It is a pleasant effect, one which occurs spontaneously to most guitarists and makes no technical demand. By contrast, the flamenco rasgueado proper is highly percussive, rhythmically exact, and not quickly learned. Regulated by a separate impulse, each finger strikes quickly at a specific group of strings and on a specific part of the beat.

The basic rasgueado is the four-finger down, which produces the following rhythmic grouping if done slowly across four strings:

To execute this, anchor your thumb on the sixth string and close the fingers into a fist. There must be full compression in the hand, with the nails tucked into the palm so that each finger thumps as it strikes outward. As you strike the triplet part of the rasgueado, make sure each finger snaps out completely before the next leaves the hand. Since the little finger is weak, it may be hard to snap to a full extension. Because of the common tendon sheath shared by the two fingers, the snap of *a* may dislodge *m*. Even so, strive for quick, percussive movements and perfect separation.

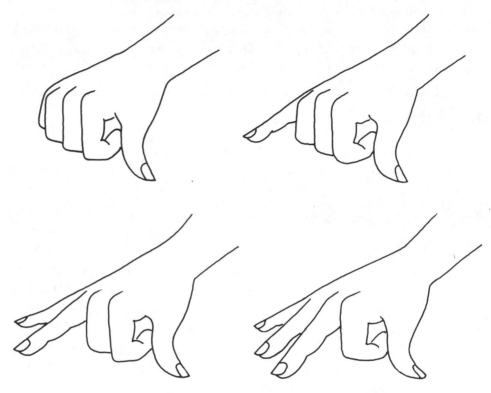

Conscientious practice of this rasgueado is tiring to the forearm; do not overstrain. As you gain control of the movement, increase the number of strings covered to all six. *Do not* attempt to strike all the strings with any one finger. Use the natural stroke of the fingers to trace an ascending pattern in which no finger plays more than three strings. The overlapping of notes creates the illusion that six strings have been struck each time. The effect will be approximately as below (brace the thumb on the soundboard, slightly back of the sixth string):

c a m i

The same illusion is the basis of the flashiest of rasgueados, the "rasgueado redondo," or continuous roll. It is impossible to play down-strokes fast enough or evenly enough for a truly continuous rasgueado.

An upstroke of the first finger must connect each downward sequence. Consequently, the division of the beat will be into even quintuplets.

The upstroke must be a light, short flick. Two strings on the upstroke are sufficient for a splendid cascade of sound once the rasgueado reaches tempo.

You will notice when you are trying to learn this rasgueado that there tends to be a hiatus between each quintuplet—a "gallop." The reason is that the little finger has not returned to the palm in time enough to be ready for its next impulse. To overcome this problem, you must return the fingers to the palm as *i* makes its downstroke; if you wait until its upstroke, you will still have a small gallop. The sensation is one of *c-i* exchange:

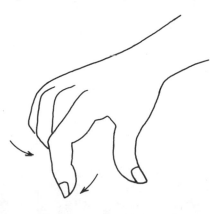

Practice the continuous rasgueado this way in distinct sequences of five to the beat. Mastery is a task of several months. There will be moments when it will come spontaneously with perfect coordination for a few seconds, then there will be a relapse.

As you gain velocity, make less effort to snap the fingers to a full extension. The fingers do not have time enough to uncurl completely at full speed, particularly the *i* finger. Be sure also that you are not pushing down into the strings; try instead for a skimming stroke.

Besides its value as a colorful device useful in numerous pieces, there is another practical benefit of learning this rasgueado. The extensor muscles which lift the fingers are developed by almost no other activity, certainly by no other musical activity. Learning a good, continuous rasgueado will develop the weak extensor muscles and thereby contribute to the overall development of the hand.

The previous techniques discussed, especially the vibrato, are a part of sensitive, imaginative musical expression on the guitar. Beyond them lies yet another realm of expression where the respective roles of thought, imagination, hearing, physical sensation, and momentary intuition are so intertwined that the whole complex is generally assumed to lie within the domain of feeling and beyond the reach of analysis.

To a large extent, this assumption is perfectly true. One cannot reduce the complexities of artistic expression to a set of rules. On the other hand, art is nearly always produced by a more conscious process than generally suspected. Particularly is this so in the area of musical performance. The ability to discriminate at finer and finer levels of muscular effort, pitch, speed, and so on is the mark of a developing musician. At the level of instrumental art, rather microscopic distinctions between nuances are possible and necessary. In the last chapter of this book, we will be concerned with some of these nuances.

CHAPTER EIGHT

The Art of Classical Guitar Playing

The real art of classical guitar playing begins and ends in listening, just as it does in playing any musical instrument. It includes the refinement of one's ear for pitch, harmony and rhythm; the marshalling of progressively more awareness of simultaneous detail; and the ability to hear oneself critically. The importance of the latter has been stated by Walter Gieseking, one of the great pianists of the twentieth century:

> Critical self-hearing is, in my opinion, by far the most important factor in all of music study. . . . only trained ears are capable of noticing the fine inexactitudes and unevennesses, the eliminating of which is necessary to a perfect technique.[1]

Gieseking is seconded in this view by leading virtuosos and teachers in all fields of music. Music schools devote time to ear-training; but as in other aspects of musicianship, the serious player must develop his own capabilities through a variety of ways.

One of the best ways is to sing as many parts of the pieces you practice as you can. There is little point in attempting to sing an arpeggio study; but what about singing, in turn, the highest, lowest, and middle voices of a polyphonic work while playing the other parts? If you have never tried this, you may find it difficult. But as an exercise to expand one's field of musical perception, it is extremely beneficial. (Aspiring orchestral conductors are expected to do this fluently with all the Bach Two-Part Inventions, alternately singing one part while playing the other.) It strengthens the interplay between the auditory and motor areas of the brain. It helps in the study of polyphonic music by clarifying the harmony. Singing also helps in learning how to phrase a melody. Even if our voices are not especially good, the shape, direction, and feeling we instinctively impart to a melody in singing can often serve as a model for the hands in playing. The habit of singing will also help the guitarist to transcend mechanical preoccupations and bring him or her nearer the goal of all instrumental expression: the illusion of song.

Taking every opportunity to play accompaniments or in ensembles will also help the guitarist. Many musical skills simply cannot be developed in isolation. We often learn best by direct example, and in this sense playing duos with flute and accompanying singers, among other possibilities, will teach a great deal of musicianship. Especially, it will impart a feel for phrase, texture, and rhythm that is hard to come by otherwise. Best of all, it will do so pleasurably! Other benefits that might be mentioned include the satisfaction of participating in the larger musical community, a better perspective on the real strengths and weaknesses of the guitar, and increased versatility.

A strategy that works surprisingly well consists of conscious listening during practice. That practice can even occur at all without listening may seem absurd, but in fact it goes on all the time. To test the truth of this, play a short piece that you know very well either or both of the following ways: (1) with your head turned to the right so that you cannot see your left hand, while most of the sound is received by the left ear; (2) with your eyes closed. The elimination of visual distraction opens the ears like nothing else. The jolt to the auditory awareness may even make the piece sound eerily unfamiliar.

You can develop a more comprehensive, more accurate auditory perception by devoting at least some time every day to practicing while listening closely but without watching the left hand. Look instead at your left knee or at the floor. Among several benefits of practicing this way can be included the more balanced "stereophonic" receptivity of the two ears and the lessening of the left hand's dependency upon the eye. Make no conscious effort to use either right- or left-hand anticipations; just listen steadily, calmly, and objectively, noting weaknesses of any kind. When you notice a weakness, repeat the passage and try to improve by better visualizing the ideal effect.

Even though in this mode of practice we are not consciously anticipating finger movements, a different kind of anticipation nonetheless is crucial—that is, anticipation of sound. We project in our inner ear an ideal effect and measure constantly the success of our playing by how well the result matches the expectation. Things that can disrupt the expectation other than outright mistakes include left-hand buzzes, nail clicks, uneven intensities, and rhythmic uncertainties. Try first for a robust, perfectly even level of tone, with no attempt at dynamic or coloristic effects. Later on, you can practice individual passages, and eventually whole pieces, for color, dynamics, and rhythmic nuance.

REFINEMENT OF TONE

To achieve a consistently even level of tone color and intensity is difficult. Two things in particular work against it. One is the difference in color from one string to another; the other is the difference between rest-stroke and free-stroke tone.

We have seen above (chapter 3, p. 37) that a downward push into the string is necessary for solid free-stroke tone. We have also seen the value of a rest stroke lightened by lowering the wrist (chapter 6, p. 76). This latter device, while intended to promote velocity in scales, also creates a more delicate sound. In fact, if you play the same scale either with rest stroke in this fashion or with the downward free stroke attack, the two treatments should sound quite similar. They can be made to sound identical. Practice scales, consecutively, with (1) heavy, accented free stroke (2) light, restrained rest stroke. This will equalize the two modes of attack. You will eventually develop a core sound that is the same whether played rest stroke or free stroke, and thus can be varied at will for contrast.

tonal extreme	tonal core	tonal extreme
delicate, light;	mezzo forte;	forte, accented;
maximum clarity	clear, yet full	maximum fullness of tone

← free stroke	rest stroke →

Whether we use free or rest stroke, however, the different tonal characteristic of each string will produce inconsistent color in the progress of a scale unless the angle of attack is varied. The same attack that gives a pleasing first-string tone will yield a muddy-sounding third string and a scratchy bass. If the attack is angled so as to produce attractive tone on the bass strings, then the higher strings will sound thin. The truth is that the angle of attack must change during a scale, from perpendicular on the sixth string to some 30 degrees on the first.

The change in angle is brought about by changes in the curvature of the wrist. The inclination of the hand, however, which is determined by forearm rotation, remains essentially unchanged.

Perpendicular nail presentation will not only narrow bass tone for better equality with the treble but will also prevent the unpleasant raking of the nail across the string winding. The leftward curving of the wrist should begin on the fourth string and increase a bit with each string change until reaching a maximum angle on the first string. In descending, reverse the process, bringing the stroke more toward the perpendicular at each string change by curving the wrist to the right. Through repeated experimentation, let the ear tell the hand how much change in position is necessary to equalize tone.

You can enhance the value of the scale even more by practicing crescendo in ascending, decrescendo in descending. Practice also with the reverse of these dynamics. Though harder, it will help train the mind and fingers for those occasions when a descending line is to be crescendo.

CONTRAST OF TONE COLOR

Since the dynamic range of the guitar is limited, expressive contrast is impossible without frequent changes in tone color. Variety in color gives life to the playing, and it is quite natural to think of the resources of the guitar in terms of an orchestral palette. Imaginative players have been doing so since the days of Giuliani and Sor.[2] Musically, this capability is the unique strong point of the instrument.

Relocations of the hand toward or away from the bridge are used for major changes in color. From the sound hole to the bridge, there are three practical positions of the hand: (1) over the sound hole; (2) just back of the sound hole, toward the bridge; (3) next to the bridge. The normal position of the hand will be the second of these positions, from which contrast may be achieved in either direction. The procedure is comparable to shifting manuals on the harpsichord or stops on the organ. It is useful to underscore structural contrasts and especially to distinguish between repeated phrases or motifs.

Small changes of curve and rotation are the means whereby the nuances of tone color are varied. As we have seen, a change in the angle of attack can be used to equalize tone on different strings. The identical technique is used to achieve contrast in tone color upon the same string or strings. From a given middle position, a quarter-inch curve of the hand toward the left will appreciably mellow the tone by inclining the nail more in the direction of the stroke. From the same middle position, a quarter-inch curve toward the right will brighten the tone by setting the nail against the direction of the stroke. Thus, a movement of no more than a half-inch, which escapes most observers, can create delicate contrasts in color without shifting the basic hand position. Even more subtle changes in thumbnail inclination produce varieties of color on the bass strings (see again the illustrations of thumb tilt on p. 47; though exaggerated, the first suggests the angle of attack for a metallic free-stroke tone, the second, for a softer tone or for rest stroke).

For greater accentuation or contrast, the two angles of finger attack can be combined with a slight propulsive gesture of the hand or forearm. When exaggerated, the result is a slice across the strings. With less propulsion, it is felt more as an emphasis of the nails to the right or left. Emphasis (or slice) to the right takes the hand momentarily away from the line of the forearm— somewhat as if screwing the cap onto a large jar, although the movement is tiny by comparison. It focuses the tone for maximum clarity by increasing the resistance of the nails. Emphasis to the left, described in chapter 7 as akin to the motion of flicking lint off one's coat, takes a small rotary movement of the forearm. The single-edge, line-of-force nail contact minimizes resistance to create a thick, mellow tone. The illustrations below show (in much exaggerated form) the change in hand position occasioned by either movement:

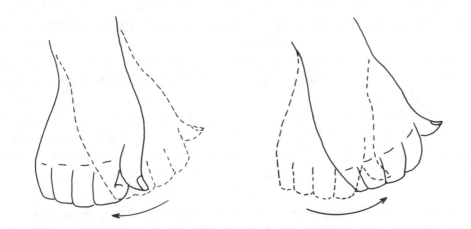

One must experiment continually to develop the feel and sound of the various possibilities as they apply to chords, arpeggios, and rest-stroke or free-stroke single notes. Of the two directions, emphasis to the left is more generally useful, since it gives a greater sonority, a "sweeter" sound. But remember that mellow sonorities have as their natural complement the frequent emphasis of the nails to the right. If sweetness is the effect of the one technique, then piquancy or spice may be regarded as the effect of the other. Together they balance each other and give variety to the style.

One version of the leftward glancing attack deserves special mention. A hallmark of Segovia's style, it places a distinctive, sonorous emphasis upon a single note. The effect is achieved in the case of single notes or pairs by a pronounced single-finger slice, whether rest stroke or free stroke. In chords, it takes the form of an arpeggiation with extra leftward emphasis upon the *a* finger. When combined with a quick release of the lower notes of a chord and vibrato upon the held highest note, the result is a warm melodic accent. (The sacrifice of lower note-values this way is often desirable and akin to the effect of chords played on the cello or violin.) The end of the first strain of Tárrega's "Adelita" contains a typical example:

CONTROL OF RHYTHM

Important as is the control of tone color, the control of rhythm is at least equally so. Besides the use of rubato and accelerando, this means controlling the placement of tones in relation to the beat. A critical and subtle issue, it is much involved in the impression of overall tone quality.

Beat, or pulse, is doubtless the most fundamental aspect of music. An amazing number of errors in performance are easily forgiven, if indeed noticed at all, as long as they are not rhythmic faults. On the other hand, the slightest rhythmic uncertainty will make an audience uncomfortable. Rhythmic vitality is more than half the reason for any effective performance.

This must not be confused with metronomic regularity, however. Expressive performance demands countless minute deviations from the beat:

> The rise and fall of the intervals of the melody, and the greater or lesser pungency of the chords of the harmony, create in the mind of the genuinely musical performer and listener a desire for tiny hurryings and lingerings such as could never be expressed in any notation . . . . These operate to modify the demands of regularity without destroying the feeling of regularity; such slight but purposeful departures from regularity suggest life as opposed to mechanism.[3]

The kind of rhythmic assurance in question, then, is the sort that can place a note before, on, or slightly after the beat at will. As in the case of tone production, Segovia's example is instructive.

Just how creative Segovia's handling of pulse is can be experienced more easily than described. Try to play in perfect time with a record. You soon find that minor rhythmic distortions are constantly employed, even when the pulse seems to be quite firm. Most noticeable are certain rubato effects. Characteristically, these take the form of a "breath pause" before an accented note which is then placed a little after the beat and held for longer than its written value. Less apparent but crucial are the frequent accelerandos; time and again, one will find the Maestro slightly rushing the beat in places where he seemed to playing right on it. Upon analysis, there is usually a musical logic in each case. But overall there is one prevailing reason for the accelerandos; they balance the more apparent rubato effects so that the beat is never really lost, although it may be hidden from time to time.

Much the same might be said of expressive performance in general, whether on the guitar or on some other instrument. But as in the case of tone production, expression must be cultivated. Particularly this is so for notes or chords that are points of accent, of arrival, or of repose. Rhythmic control of such emphases is very difficult; first, because the beat will always tend to assert its dominance in reflex playing; second, because under the stress of performance, there is a natural tendency to rush. The following examples from Sor are typical:

"Variations on a Theme of Mozart," 1st variation

Estudio 2, end

"Variations on La Folia," beginning

In the first example, if the variation is played at an appropriately brilliant tempo, the scale from B up to A tends to fly out of control; consequently, the arrival at the A may sound more desperate than graceful. Though the technical level of the second example is less, the rhythmic control needed at the cadence is quite similar. The final C of the melody must be held back very slightly to sound rhythmically relaxed; however, the drive of the beat urges a vulgar sforzando accent instead. In the third example, the pressure of tempo is much less than in the preceding examples, but yet the problem of rhythmic control is similar. If the suspended E is to be heard as the focal point of the initial motif, there must be some crescendo in the first measure and a restraint of the pulse before the accent.

Since the rhythmic control in these cases—and countless others like them—is so subtle, it may seem more the product of intuition and of taste than of conscious intent. The control can definitely be learned, however. The secret is a form of exaggeration in practice. Try to interrupt the beat in each case with a complete stop before the note or chord of emphasis. To realize the full benefit of this practice technique, you should in fact pause at the exact moment of execution, and only after the preparation has been accomplished. Since this frustration of a reflex impulse is extremely difficult at first, try it only at the slowest speeds. As you gain control, try to achieve a comparable restraint at tempi approaching performance. In time, the unconscious motor centers will absorb much of the effort of restraint (and much of the attendant feeling of frustration). Eventually, one will be left with an enhanced sense of rhythm; of interpretive power; of freedom from the tyranny of the beat, or more exactly, from the tyranny of uncontrolled reflexes.[4]

DEVELOPING THE LINE: THINKING UPBEATS

Various kinds of musical awareness go into good phrasing. Among other things, they include sensitivity to rhythmic stress, melodic contour, harmonic activity, points of energy and repose within the line, and so on. For the most part, such matters are beyond the scope of this book. However, there is an important exception, the development of a linear melodic sense.

Consider playing the Estudio 6 by Sor:

Most players will tend unconsciously to stress the long notes in both parts. In fact, unless there is a conscious effort to avoid it, the result may sound like this: la FA (re La), fa MI (la So), mi RE (re Fa), fa LA (re Fa), etc. If so, it will merely typify a common tendency to overplay metric accents. Assuredly, the sense of rhythm in a piece often calls for stress at the natural accent points. Just as often, though, this is not the case. The Sor example above speaks for hundreds of such situations. Clearly, what is wanted is a stress pattern in performance that follows the general melodic contour. Therefore, between the first and the last F sharp in the treble part, there should be a decrescendo, while the last F sharp itself should be accented. This means, in turn, that the downbeats must be deemphasized in favor of heavier stress on the upbeats so as to produce a steady, even melodic flow.

If one is used to overplaying downbeats unconsciously, it is practically impossible to achieve the desired evenness just by consciously trying for evenness. Almost always, the line will still sound chopped up by metric accents. As in so many other cases, the objective is attained by a form of deliberate exaggeration—here, by reversing the natural accent pattern in practice. That is, overplay the upbeats; underplay the downbeats: LA fa (Re la), FA mi (La so), MI re (Re fa), FA la, etc. Although this will probably sound outrageously unmusical to the player first attempting it, as he gains control of the practice technique, his ear will begin to accept emphasis on upbeats as fundamentally musical. As the process of ear accommodation continues, he will find that his sense of phrasing is being sharpened.

He may also find that his left-hand fluency is being improved because there is a special application of the above principle to fingerboard shifts. Because of the sympathetic neural linkage, an increased effort in one hand tends to produce, involuntarily, an increased effort by the other. Thus, it is very hard to play *forte* while keeping the left-hand touch light; conversely, lessening the volume encourages the left hand to expend less energy. This principle can be applied in a general way to the improvement of fluency (see pages 32 and 76.) If we apply it specifically to shifting, we will see that often a technical rough spot can be smoothed over by a scrupulous attention to dynamics.

Most typically, a shift will fall on a metric accent and will furthermore be preceded by an upbeat whose function is rhythmic and melodic anticipation. The following examples from the Gigue of the First Lute Suite by Bach are characteristic:

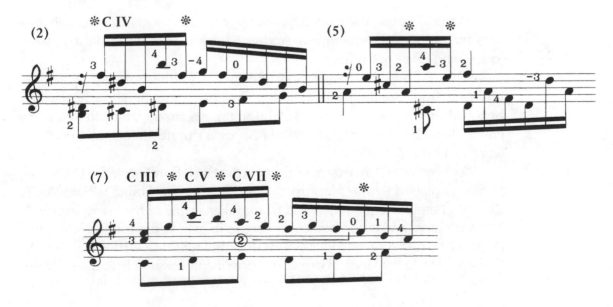

In each case (marked by asterisks), the smoothness of the shift will be affected by how we hear the upbeat. If we hear the upbeat harmonically and metrically, it will seem part of a chord on an unemphatic part of the beat. We will mentally connect it with the preceding downbeat and underplay it while summoning our energy for the shift. The result will be overemphasis by the right hand on the downbeat following, the anticipation of which will also increase the energy expended by the left hand during the shift.

Conversely, if we hear the upbeat rhythmically and melodically, we will mentally connect it with the downbeat following. Thus understood, it will seem natural to treat it as a "push" to the downbeat by accenting it. With a corresponding underemphasis of the downbeat after the shift, the result will be a much smoother connection than if the downbeat is accented. The deliberate restraint of the right hand at the moment of shift automatically lessens the effort of the left hand. The jolt of the shift seems absorbed into the note preceding it, while the left hand seems to arrive at the new position as if by parachute.

The elbow anticipation discussed above in chapter 2 (p. 21 ff.) must not be overlooked in this style of practice. However, for the player who has learned to use that important form of anticipation, the further association of the shift with a right-hand dynamic device and the incorporation of the whole within the musical upbeat impulse will represent one further step toward the elusive goal of relaxed, accurate performance in which the ear seems to guide the hand.

EXPRESSIVE NUANCES: SEGOVIA'S EXAMPLE

Beyond doubt, the main influence upon classical guitar playing in this century has been the example of Andrés Segovia. There is hardly a guitarist today who does not reflect it.

This is not to suggest that Segovia's unquestionably individual interpretations are a universal model. They do, however, show how much beauty there can be in the sound of the guitar. It is surely fitting, therefore, to conclude with some close analysis of Segovia's performance as a guide to what can be done.

As appropriate an example as any is the Bach Sarabande for Violin in B minor as played by the Maestro on his "Segovia on Stage" album (MCA 2531). The piece is a familiar and beautiful example of his many fine Bach transcriptions, and is comparatively easy to follow. Examining its first strain measure by measure, and in a kind of stop-the-action slow motion, will help to demonstrate the kinds of expressive possibilities available to the sensitive player.

Measure 1. The first chord is arpeggiated with rightward nail emphasis; the second is delayed slightly, broadly arpeggiated, and sliced to the left for warmer tone. The emphatic second beat, in keeping with Sarabande style, delays the onset of the third, whose chord is arpeggiated less. The single E is rushed slightly and played rest stroke, with leftward emphasis so as not to sound weak compared with the preceding chords.

Measure 2. The chord, retarded to provide space for the preceding E to "breathe," is played without arpeggiation (note, however, the vibrato). It is held for less than its full dotted value. Why? Because on the violin, the melody note F sharp would swell and clearly delineate the second beat. Since this is impossible on the guitar, Segovia abbreviates the chord just a bit so as not to lose the momentum of the piece. The three eighth notes that conclude the measure are rushed slightly, perhaps to offset the gravity of the first measure and to emphasize melodic direction.

Measure 3. The leap from B to E makes the latter rather the more accented, and we hear it as an upbeat to the D of the strong second beat. The D is firmly accented, with the bass taken clearly before the beat. In contrast to this emphasis, the last two notes of the measure are treated with a light staccato, as upbeats for the next measure.

Measure 4. The A sharp is given the mellow tone of a leftward slice since it is a prominent point of repose. The bass F sharp is muted and shortened to an eighth note to finish the phrase and to permit an expressive left-hand fingering of the next entry. Like its counterpart in measure 2, this motif is rushed slightly and played staccato (by the thumb, with clear nail tone). The darker fifth-string color of the final E smooths the connection with the D of the next measure.

Measure 5. The first two chords are punched out with a heavy accent, and the second of them is retarded to make room for the resonance of the first. The G on the third beat is accented with a leftward slice of the *i* finger, emphasizing the dramatic value of the note as the lowest in the first strain.

Measure 6. The accentuation of the first chord is vigorous, corresponding to the energy of the tritone leap in the melody from the preceding G. The music builds from here to the final cadence. The C sharp of the second beat is abbreviated; the D, rushed in consequence, is played rest stroke and treated unexpectedly as a pronounced staccato tone. As in measure 2, the reason is to provide forward momentum, here to the harmonically active F sharp 7 chord of the third beat. The chord itself is heard as an accented upbeat to the next measure.

Measures 7 and 8. The B minor chord of the first beat is arpeggiated; leftward slice emphasizes the suspended E. The open-string E of the second beat has a nail-focused metallic nuance (characteristic of Segovia's use of open strings). The D on the second half of the beat is staccato, in anticipation of the accented C sharp of the third beat. Finally, the cadence chord in measure 8 is retarded for emphasis and executed with a flesh-only thumb sweep.

Summary. Despite the variety of detail, the overall impression is that Segovia is motivated here by three primary aesthetic concerns: to keep up the forward momentum of the piece at all times, to achieve contrast through the use of varied accentuations and colors, and to make each note speak with the best resonance possible.

The description above bears about the same relation to the performance as does a recipe to the actual eating of haute cuisine. And of course, no one thinks about music in such a piecemeal way while actually performing it. Many details of the kind spelled out above will be assimilated intuitively within a performance concept whose main concerns are melodic direction and contour, harmonic texture, and rhythmic accent.

The fact remains, however, that the recorded performance more than bears out the detailed explication, here and elsewhere. And, if during the actual performance conscious awareness of such minutiae is impractical, in the preparation of the piece, it is not only practical but obligatory if real instrumental art is the object. The unglamorous truth, so difficult sometimes to accept, is that the great artists are also thoughtful, painstaking workers. The achievement of any competence whatever requires a discipline; the higher the level, the more arduous the discipline. If the goal really matters, then it will seem to justify the effort.

But perhaps in this context the distinction between ends and means is spurious. Why do we practice a scale? To answer by the book, so that our playing will become faster and more coordinated; and to continue the catechism, so that we can play pieces presently beyond us, and in turn perform them, become bored with them, look for satisfaction to higher levels of the repertoire, seek to improve technique to reach them, and thus once again return to the practice of scales. The circle is not really vicious; it is simply the only one there is.

The truth is that we play, and practice, because we want to, and find the activity gratifying. It is perhaps significant that in more than one language one *plays* an instrument, whether for fun or for profit. A brilliant performance for a large audience is an exhiliarating experience, especially when a fee is involved; but so is the discovery one morning that one can play the three-octave G scale six metronome points higher than yesterday. In either case, we have met a challenge, surmounted it, and experienced as the happy reward a sensation of personal growth. The study of the classical guitar can be a constantly unfolding panorama of such challenges, filled with possibilities of discovery—and self-discovery.

APPENDIX:

A Practice Checklist

The outline below summarizes the main points in this book and offers a few further suggestions for beneficial practice. It may be useful to the reader either as a topic index or as a "reminder list." The topic headings generally follow the sequence of chapters; numbers in parentheses refer to the relevant pages of the text.

I. Seating
   A. Position of guitar (10)
      1. Instrument rests squarely on left thigh
      2. Neck is inclined inward (toward left hand)
      3. Neck makes shallow angle (30–35 degrees) with floor
   B. Legs (9-10)
      1. Left leg is only moderately elevated (depending on length of torso and height of chair)
      2. Right leg is poised on ball of foot
      3. Legs grip inward to stabilize
   C. Torso (11)
      1. Avoid slump; spine is straight
      2. Avoid shoulder hunching
      3. Lean into the instrument
      4. Note that center of gravity is to the left
   D. Arm (11)
      1. Forearm, not upper arm, rests on guitar
      2. Hand falls over strings with no muscular effort of the arm
      3. Deltoid keeps arm from slumping without hunching the shoulder

II. Left-hand position
   A. The arm (14; 22 ff.)
      1. Forearm and hand are aligned as for normal grip
      2. Upper arm is sufficiently away from body to permit the above alignment, but without winging
      3. Shifts begin with appropriate elbow movement; elbow also moves in and out to support reaches with 3 and 4
      4. "Play" in rotation of forearm and flex of wrist support various finger placements
   B. The hand (15 ff.; 29)
      1. Knuckles are generally parallel to fingerboard
      2. Thumb generally opposes second finger, except for bars, where it opposes the first
      3. Minimum thumb pressure is desirable
      4. Tip of thumb is turned back and joints locked
      5. There is no outward rotation of palm during shifts
      6. Muscles in heel of hand contract to support the action of fourth finger, particularly in slurs
   C. The fingers (15 ff.)
      1. Strong unbroken arch requires vertical approach of tips
      2. Lateral separation at knuckle is pronounced except for close spacings
      3. Minimal lift restrains excess movement
      4. Minimal pressure helps prevent fatigue, sluggish movement, and toppling over of guide fingers
      5. Bars include contraction of middle joint: full contraction for partial bar, partial contraction for full bar

III. Right-hand position
   A. The hand (36 ff.)
      1. Wrist is gently arched, knuckles prominent, fingers compressed (Ping-Pong ball held in the palm helps to form the position)
      2. Knuckles are positioned almost vertically over tips for most playing; velocity scales are the main exception
      3. Sensations of weight and support from the arm are transmitted through the hand to the strings
   B. The fingers (41 ff.)
      1. Joint fixation from knuckle to tip makes for most efficient transmission of force; minimal play in tip joint
      2. Nails engage strings simultaneously with flesh contact
      3. Strokes are divided into preparatory and execution phases in deliberate practice
      4. Push, rather than pluck, is the basis of free stroke

C. The thumb (44)
1. Approach is at an angle of some 45 degrees with string
2. Tip is turned back for best presentation of nail
3. Division of stroke is same as for fingers in B. (2) and (3) above
4. Varieties of length and flexibility necessitate minor modifications of overall hand position

IV. Coordination of the hands
A. Staccato practice necessary for coordination (61 ff.)
1. Percussive note formations are inherent to guitar
2. Staccato places note beginnings with rhythmic exactitude and softens the attack
3. Articulation allows left hand to move more nimbly
4. Right-left impulses are synchronized and therefore more efficient
B. Arpeggios (64)
1. All clear ascending figures are prepared simultaneously as for a chord
2. Execute-prepare impulses overlap in the case of descending or single-string figures;

$$\left. \begin{array}{l} \text{execute } a \\ \text{prepare } m \end{array} \right\} \qquad \left. \begin{array}{l} \text{execute } m \\ \text{prepare } i \end{array} \right\}$$

C. Scales (71)
1. Within a position, preparation of right-hand fingers coincides with fall of left-hand fingers
2. In shifts, right-hand preparation anticipates and masks left-hand movements
D. Chords; homophonic and contrapunctal textures (77)
1. Right-hand fingers block out their prepared positions before left hand moves
2. In the case of difficult shifts, preparation takes more time and can be considered rhythmically as an upbeat to the new chord
3. Since most music consists of combinations of scales, chords, and arpeggios, constant combination of all the above forms of preparation is typical
E. Velocity in scales (74)
1. Use metronome and practice scales in distinct rhythmic groupings of triplets and sixteenths
2. Keep thumb on a bass string for support
3. Use lower wrist than for ordinary playing
4. Keep tip joints firm; play from the tip, as if scratching

5. Use decisive staccato preparations for controlled playing; be especially careful that preparation is decisive at points of string change
6. Abandon staccato preparation for peak velocity playing; try for an unbroken wave of notes

V. Expression
  A. Slurs (87)
    1. Variable stress is created, as in speech
    2. Improved fluency in scalewise passages results
  B. Vibrato (90)
    1. Pendulum or seesaw momentum of the forearm is in a strictly sidewise plane, like shaking a bottle
    2. Intensity is appropriate to note—never excessive
    3. Lateral-bend (finger) vibrato in lowest and highest fingerboard positions is used
  C. Arpeggiation of chords (96)
    1. Fingers are more relaxed than for articulate arpeggios
    2. Variable spreading is possible, from broad to nearly simultaneous
    3. Broken chords generally begin before the beat so that melody falls on the beat
    4. Arpeggiation sometimes clarifies texture in contrapuntal music
  D. Rhythmic nuances (110)
    1. Pulse is not metronomic; minor rubatos and accelerandos are constant in good playing
    2. Occasional "breath pauses" help at phrase divisions, before accents, or at a difficult shift
  E. Nuances of tone color (107)
    1. Free- and rest-stroke tone should be nearly equal, except for deliberate contrast
    2. Angle of nail presentation varies: emphasis to left for richness or warmth; to right, for clarity or brightness
    3. Hand is moved toward or away from bridge for further contrast

VI. Slow practice schemes
  A. Left-hand anticipation (31)
    1. Visualize each new formation before leaving the present one
    2. Physically anticipate where possible with free fingers, guide fingers, or pivot fingers
    3. Use appropriate elbow anticipation for shifts

      4. Move as economically as possible, with tips always pointed to fingerboard

      5. Concentrate on restraint and liquid quality of finger movement

      6. Play very softly, with no attempt at right hand preparation

  B. Right-hand anticipation (71 ff.)

      1. Watch right hand, not left

      2. Experience separate sensations of preparation and execution for each stroke

      3. Listen for distinct staccato; the more distinct, the more controlled

      4. Be especially careful when shifting that the right hand has prepared before the left hand begins to move

      5. Play decisively and forcefully

  C. Anticipation of sound (106 ff.)

      1. Watch neither right nor left hand; look at knee or floor

      2. Make no conscious attempt to prepare right- or left-finger settings; just listen intently and objectively

      3. Try for even intensity; consider as mistakes any imperfections in tone or rhythm, as well as extraneous noises

      4. Practice individual passages and whole pieces for color, for dynamic effect (crescendo, accent), and for rhythmic vitality

  D. Upbeat emphasis and control of rhythm (110 ff.)

      1. Emphasize upbeats generally to avoid playing with heavy metric emphasis

      2. Emphasize especially where upbeats clearly serve as melodic or rhythmic anticipation

      3. When the upbeat precedes a shift, synchronize with the shift impulse; try to feel the right hand pushing the left to the new position; underplay the downbeat

      4. Pause before notes or chords of emphasis

VII. General musical development

  A. Sing all the parts you can in the pieces you play, both by themselves and while playing the other parts

  B. Spend at least some time each week in sight-reading. The connection between facility in sight-reading and facility in playing is very strong

  C. Practice new music without the guitar by reading silently and fingering mentally

  D. Use a tape recorder occasionally to provide an objective check on your playing

  E. Seek opportunities to perform in ensemble settings, especially with other instruments

F. Listen intently and repeatedly to the best recordings of pieces you work on; try to understand in detail what the interpretation consists of

G. Attend as many live symphonic concerts as you can; listen deliberately for orchestral color, rhythmic nuance, dynamics. Beethoven is said to have called the guitar "a small orchestra"; an appreciation of the possibilities implied by the compliment underlies the finest playing.

Selected Bibliography

The annotated listing below is intended as a practical guide to the reader. It is by no means exhaustive. The works listed are those which were helpful in the development of the ideas in this book or which, in the author's experience, offer useful exercises for the improvement of guitar technique.

Baines, Anthony (ed.), *Musical Instruments Through the Ages.* 2d ed. New York: Walker, 1976. For anyone interested in the comparison of various instrumental techniques, provides a good background on the history of the instruments themselves.

Barlow, Wilfred. *The Alexander Technique.* New York: Knopf, 1976. Describes a system of spinal relaxation and postural balance which has attracted the attention of string teachers.

Bobri, Vladimir. *130 Daily Studies for the Classic Guitar.* New York: Franco Colombo, 1967. Varied material for the practice of arpeggios; modernizes and improves upon the 120 Daily Studies by Giuliani.

Boyden, David D. *The History of Violin Playing from Its Origins to 1761.* London: Oxford, 1965. Definitive study and a model of the highest musical scholarship. What Boyden has to say is informative generally, but there are specific parallels that the guitarist can draw to his own instrument.

Carlevaro, Abel. *Serie Didactica para Guitarra.* Cuadernos 3 and 4, *Tecnica de la Mano Izquierda.* Buenos Aires: Barry, 1969, 1975. Books 3 and 4 of this important series present the most sophisticated available study material for the left hand. Many ingenious exercises in contraction and separation, in cross-board movements, and in various kinds of shifting.

Donington, Robert. *The Interpretation of Early Music.* London: Faber & Faber, 1963. Authoritative study in the field of its title.

Duarte, John W. *The Bases of Classic Guitar Technique.* London: Novello, 1975. Brief, lucid outline of the general principles of hand position and use.

_____ *Foundation Studies in Classic Guitar Technique.* London: Novello, 1966. Concisely presented but comprehensive exercises in scale patterns, slurs, and arpeggios; imaginative use of chords for arpeggios.

Galamian, Ivan. *Principles of Violin Playing and Teaching*. Englewood Cliffs, N.J. Prentice-Hall, 1962. Practical and empirical in orientation, with occasional applicability to guitar playing.

Gerig, Reginald R. *Famous Pianists and Their Technique*. Washington and New York: Robert B. Luce, 1974. Surveys the history of piano technique, with generous quotation of historical sources. Illuminates the controversy at the beginning of this century out of which came efforts to put piano technique on a more scientific basis.

Keller, Hermann. *Phrasing and Articulation*. Translated by Leigh Gerdine. New York: Norton, 1965. About the only general study in the field of its title that is commonly available in English.

Kochevitsky, George. *The Art of Piano Playing*. Princeton, N.J.: Summy-Birchard Music,1967. Highly informative, authoritative discussion of the neurophysiology of piano playing, with direct relevance to all forms of instrumental technique. A necessary complement to Ortmann (see below).

Mantel, Gerhard. *Cello Technique*. Translated by Barbara H. Thiem. Bloomington: Indiana University, 1975. The clinical detail in which all aspects of cello technique is discussed contains time and again useful parallels to guitar technique. A major book.

Menuhin, Yehudi. *Theme and Variations*. New York: Stein and Day, 1972. Inspiring musical philosophy of one of the great masters. Emphasizes the importance of "balance" at all levels of thought, feeling, and technique.

Newman, William S. *The Pianist's Problems*. 3d ed. New York: Harper and Row, 1974. So perceptive, wide-ranging, and musically relevant that it sheds light on the guitarist's problems as well.

Noad, Frederick M. *Solo Guitar Playing*. 2d ed. New York: Schirmer, 1976. Of the many basic methods available, perhaps the most well-rounded. Sound technical presentation, excellent variety of pieces and exercises; goes well into the intermediate level.

Norton, M.D. Herter. *The Art of String Quartet Playing*. New York: Simon and Schuster, 1962. Contains much good advice on phrasing and interpretation.

Nurmi, Ruth G. *A Plain and Easy Introduction to the Harpsichord*. Albuquerque: University of New Mexico, 1974. Since the mechanics of sound production for the harpsichord parallel that for the guitar, this comprehensive guide to harpsichord playing offers some instructive analogies for guitar.

Ortmann, Otto. *The Physiological Mechanics of Piano Technique*. Baltimore, 1929. Reprint. New York: Dutton, 1962. A study without parallel in the field of its title. The muscles used and the physical tasks involved are much the same in guitar as in piano playing. Consequently, the book illuminates the technical concerns of guitarists.

Polnauer, Frederick, and Marks, Morton. *Senso-Motor Study and Its Application to Violin Playing*. Urbana: American String Teachers' Association, 1964. Does somewhat the same for the violin that Ortmann did for the piano.

Rudolf, Max. *The Grammar of Conducting*. New York: Schirmer, 1950. Generally informative guide to orchestral performance, but also offers pointed lessons in the discipline of "thinking ahead," an absolute necessity for conductors.

Scholes, Percy A. *The Oxford Companion to Music*. 9th ed. London: Oxford, 1955. Perhaps the best all-around single volume reference work.

Scott, Charles Kennedy. *Madrigal Singing*. London: Oxford, 1931. Genial guide to group singing that contains valuable advice on phrasing.

Seashore, Carl. *The Psychology of Music*. New York: McGraw-Hill, 1938. Important study by the century's foremost researcher in the field of acoustics and musical aesthetics. Chapters 5, 8, and 17 deal with instrumental timbre and vibrato and are especially informative.

Segovia, Andrés. *Diatonic Major and Minor Scales*. Washington, D.C.: Columbia Music, 1953. Still the standard fingering of two- and three-octave scales.

_____. *Slur Exercises and Chromatic Octaves*. Washington, D.C.: Columbia Music, 1975. Supplements the slur exercises in this book.

Shearer, Aaron. *Scale Pattern Studies for Guitar*. New York: Franco Colombo, 1965. Abundant position exercises in all keys supplement the Segovia scales by teaching conceptual command of the fingerboard; also good practice in sight-reading.

Sor, Fernando. *Method for the Spanish Guitar.* Translated by A. Merrick. London: n.d. Reprint. New York: Da Capo Press, 1971. Of interest for the quality of analysis in its substantial expository text; if dated, nonetheless thoughtful and intelligent.

Weisberg, Arthur. *The Art of Wind Playing.* New York: Macmillan, 1975. Informative book by the dean of American woodwind teachers. Especially valuable in its clear, meticulous analysis of various kinds of articulation.

Notes

Chapter One

1. See Reginald R. Gerig, *Famous Pianists and Their Technique* (Washington and New York: Robert B. Luce, 1974) for a full discussion of the controversy.

2. Arnold M. Schultz, *The Riddle of the Pianist's Finger and Its Relation to a Touch Scheme* [1936] (New York: Schirmer, 1949), p. 28.

3. Gerhard Mantel, *Cello Technique* [1965], tr. Barbara Thiem (Bloomington: Indiana University, 1975), p. 35.

4. Its origin is in the central nervous system, and as such it is susceptible to psychological influence. The distinction between physiological and psychological here is a practical one. For a thorough and illuminating discussion of this complex matter, see George Kochevitsky, *The Art of Piano Playing* (Princeton, N.J.: Summy-Birchard Music, 1967), pp. 21–23.

5. See, for example, Kochevitsky, pp. 52–53.

6. For a thorough discussion of the anatomical and mechanical principles, see Otto R. Ortmann, *The Physiological Mechanics of Piano Technique* [1929] (New York: Dutton, 1962).

7. An unorthodox but practical device to give even more positive support is the addition of two short strips of gummed electrical friction tape to the underside of the instrument at its waist. This will prevent the small wobble which otherwise is practically inevitable when the fabric of trouser or gown has a high finish. The tape is unobtrusive and will not mar the varnish of the instrument, although it may put a smudge on light-colored fabric!

8. This is hardly to say that such efforts are not worth serious consideration. For example, the system of spinal relaxation developed by F.M. Alexander (see Bibliography, under Wilfred Barlow) has generated some real interest among string players; see Eckhart Richter, "Good Sitting Balance in Cello Playing," *American String Teacher*, XXVI, Nos. 2 and 3 (Spring, Summer, 1976), 28 ff. The study procedures in this book tend, in fact, to be supported by Alexander's emphasis on the need for better awareness of the *means* whereby physical activities are performed, as opposed to blind preoccupation with the *ends* toward which they are directed. Alexander technique is not, however, oriented particularly toward the improvement of musical performance. Rather, it is a general system of physiotherapy concerned with tensions and disorders arising from chronic postural faults. A recently-published "do-it-yourself" guide is *The Alexander Technique,* by Sarah Barker (New York: Bantam Books, 1978).

Chapter Two

1. Usually a bar of five or even four strings is indicated in the music as a full bar; sometimes, though, the four-string bar is considered to be a "half-bar." In many editions, no distinction is made between partial and full bars. The player must experiment to determine the proper number of strings to cover. The symbols used also vary widely. A partial bar at the second fret, for example, may be indicated among the following ways: ½CII, ½B2, MC2, ¢2, ♭II, ½II.

2. Mantel, *Cello Technique*, p. 32. Mantel's whole discussion of movement, pp. 3–64, is most illuminating.

3. Abel Carlevaro (see Bibliography) has devised numerous exercises to develop this awareness. Ingenious and comprehensive, they should be consulted by the serious student.

4. The subject of embellishment is far more extensive than can be covered in a manual of instrumental technique. It is properly an aspect of the history of music performance, a matter for scholarly investigation—and debate. See, for an authoritative treatment, Robert Donington, *The Interpretation of Early Music* (London: Faber & Faber, 1963). *The Oxford Companion to Music* (see Bibliography) has a useful table of common ornaments, pp. lii–lvi.

5. For further single-string patterns, *Slur Exercises* by Andrés Segovia (see Bibliography) is recommended.

6. The physiological link between mental imagery and muscular activity has been proved by experiment: "Various people of the behaviorist school have suggested that it is impossible even to think of an activity without causing contractions in the muscles which, enlarged, would produce the actual movement." Wilfrid Barlow, *The Alexander Technique* (New York: Knopf, 1976), pp. 127–128.

Chapter Three

1. A slight exception is that minority who, influenced directly or indirectly by the outstanding examples of the late Ida Presti and her husband Alexandre Lagoya, play off the bridge side of their fingernails. To do so requires a little more turn of the wrist and more separation between thumb and fingers than is normally desirable. This does not mean that the position is unworkable; its use includes a few players of international repute. An uncommonly flexible wrist seems to go with preference of this position, and of course the fingernails must be filed quite differently than for the standard manner of touch.

2. Cf. John W. Duarte, *The Bases of Classic Guitar Technique* (London: Novello, 1975), p. 14. I am indebted in a general way to much of Mr. Duarte's lucid, concise analysis of hand position and use.

3. Yehudi Menuhin, *Violin: Six Lessons* (New York: Viking, 1972), p. 114.

Chapter Four

1. Carl Seashore's pioneer study in this field is still authoritative. See *The Psychology of Music* (New York, 1938; New York: Dover Reprints, 1967), Chapters 5 and 17 in particular.

2. See Sheila M. Nelson, *The Violin and Viola* (New York: Norton, 1972), p. 253; also Arthur Weisberg, *The Art of Wind Playing* (New York: Macmillan, 1975), p. 28.

3. Acoustically, it seems to be the product of a predominant third partial; see J. Jovicic, "Analyse Harmonique des Tons Produits des Différentes Manières d'Excitation de la

Corde de la Guitare," *Acustica*, XIX (1967/68), 103–07. "Good tone," for the guitar as for the violin, presumes a symmetrical decrease of intensity within the overtone series; see Seashore, *The Psychology of Music*, pp. 216–217.

Chapter Five

1. See Weisberg, *The Art of Wind Playing,* for the most comprehensive discussion of articulation available. Weisberg's analysis includes numerous diagrams of specific woodwind attacks to which, in a general way, I am indebted here.

2. *Legato* (It.. *legare*, to bind) and *staccato* (It. *distaccare*, to detach) are opposites. The ideal legato is a seamless juncture between consecutive tones. Staccato describes notes articulated and cut short so as to receive approximately half their literal value. *Détaché* (Fr. *détacher*, to detach) implies both less separation and a less consonantal attack. It refers to separate tonguings or bow strokes with no attempt to shorten notes. *Spiccato* (It. *spiccare*, to pluck, or to pronounce distinctly) is a particular bowed version of staccato produced by a light bounce of the bow. *Martelé* or *martellato* (Fr., It., hammered) is sometimes used to describe a sforzato woodwind attack, but it is primarily a bow term whose affinity with a good prepared attack on the guitar is very strong. It takes a pressure set of the bow as a separate impulse. The "push" into the string and the heavy articulation produced resembles in technique and effect an accented rest stroke on the guitar.

3. Weisberg, *The Art of Wind Playing*, pp. 18, 24.

4. Ivan Galamian, *Principles of Violin Playing and Teaching* (Englewood Cliffs, N.J.: Prentice-Hall, 1962), p. 71.

5. Kochevitsky, *The Art of Piano Playing,* p. 25.

6. Leopold Mozart, *A Treatise on the Fundamental Principles of Violin Playing* [Augsburg, 1756], tr. Editha Knocker (London: Oxford, 1948), p. 87.

7. David Boyden, *The History of Violin Playing from Its Origins to 1761* (London: Oxford, 1965), pp. 498-499.

Chapter Six

1. Ortmann, *The Physiological Mechanics of Piano Technique,* pp. 64–65, 71.

2. Ibid., pp. 226-227.

3. Mantel, *Cello Technique,* pp. 51–53.

4. Weisberg, *The Art of Wind Playing*, pp. 132–133.

5. See Kochevitsky, *The Art of Piano Playing*, pp. 21–23, for the neurological aspects of the musical learning process.

6. C.P.E. Bach, for example, says that notes which are neither staccato nor legato should last for half (!) their indicated value, while distinctly staccato notes are still shorter. See his *Essay on the True Art of Playing Keyboard Instruments* [Berlin, 1753], tr. William J. Mitchell (London: Cassell, 1949), pp. 154, 157.

Chapter Seven *Expressive Devices* .

1. See Donington, *The Interpretation of Early Music*, pp. 167–170.

2. See, for a particularly severe attack, Percy Scholes, "Tremolo and Vibrato," *The Oxford Companion to Music* (9th ed.; London: Oxford, 1965), p. 1044.

3. Carl E. Seashore (ed.), *Objective Analysis of Musical Performance (Studies in the Psychology of Music*, Vol. IV; Iowa City: University of Iowa Press, 1936).

4. See Mantel, *Cello Technique*, pp. 97–105, 194–195, for an exhaustive analysis of the anatomical and mechanical principles involved. The type of cello vibrato Mantel prefers has virtually the same technique as a guitar vibrato.

5. The most common names for the little finger in Spanish, *meñique* and *pequeño*, have the same initial letter as another finger. *C* here stands for *chico*, which is also sometimes used to designate the little finger.

Chapter Eight

1. Walter Gieseking, Foreword to *The Shortest Way to Pianistic Perfection*, by [Karl] Leimert-[Walter] Gieseking, (Philadelphia: Theodore Presser, 1932), p. 5.

2. See Sor's discussion of the possibilities in his *Method for the Spanish Guitar*, tr. A. Merrick, (London: R. Cocks and Co., n.d.), pp. 15–18.

3. Scholes, *The Oxford Companion to Music*, p. 877.

4. See Kochevitsky, *The Art of Piano Playing*, pp. 25–26, for discussion of how this form of practice trains the musical reflexes of the central nervous system.